Navigating Your Future

Navigating Your Future

The Principles of Student Success

James G. Beierlein
The Pennsylvania State University

Barbara K. Wade
The Pennsylvania State University

Houghton Mifflin Company   Boston   New York

Director of College Survival: Barbara A. Heinssen
Assistant Editor: Shani B. Fisher
Editorial Assistant: Jonathan T. Wolf
Senior Production/Design Coordinator: Sarah Ambrose
Senior Manufacturing Coordinator: Marie Barnes
Marketing Manager: Barbara LeBuhn

Cover image provided by EyeWire Inc.

College Survival
A Program of Houghton Mifflin Company
2075 Foxfield Drive, Suite 100
St. Charles, IL 60174

Text credits: Inside cover and pp. 14–16: *Measurement and Evaluation in Teaching*, Fifth Edition by Gronlund, Norman E. Copyright © 1985. Reprinted by permission of Prentice-Hall, Inc., Upper Saddle River, NJ; pp. 93–94: "Index of Reading Awareness" reprinted by permission of the author; pp. 123–124: Reprinted by permission of Lynn Z. Bloom and Martin Bloom. Adapted from "Becoming an Effective Self-Critic," *Journal of English Teaching Techniques*, I:3 (Fall, 1968), p. 8; pp. 151–152: John Dewey, *How We Think*. Copyright © 1933 by D.C. Heath and Company. Reprinted by permission of Houghton Mifflin Company; p. 161: Mind map designed by Ellen Taricani, Penn State University; p. 172: Screen shot reprinted with the permission of Penn State University Student Affairs Career Services; p. 177: Resume used with permission from Penn State University Student Affairs Career Services.

Photo credits: p. 1: © Bonnie Kamin/PhotoEdit; p. 3: © Tony Freeman/PhotoEdit; p. 7: © Rudi Von Briel/PhotoEdit; p. 23: © Michael Newman/PhotoEdit; p. 26: © Gary A. Conner/PhotoEdit; p. 29: © David Young-Wolff/PhotoEdit; p. 40: © Christopher S. Johnson/Stock, Boston; p. 42: © David Young-Wolff/PhotoEdit; p. 65: © Joe Sohm/The Image Works; p. 67: © Lara Jo Regan/Liaison Agency; p. 81: © 2002 Andy Sacks/Stone; p. 83: © Esbin-Anderson/The Image Works; p. 85: © Barbara Alper/Stock, Boston; p. 89: © Robert Daemmrich/The Image Works; p. 103: © Gary A. Conner/PhotoEdit; p. 120: © David Young-Wolff/PhotoEdit; p. 125: © David Young-Wolff/PhotoEdit; p. 129: © Spencer Grant/PhotoEdit; p. 137: © 2002 Terry Vine/Stone; p. 138: © Michael Newman/PhotoEdit; p. 139: © Margot Granitsas/The Image Works; p. 141: © Jeff Greenberg/Photo Researchers; p. 142: © Susan Van Etten/PhotoEdit; p. 143: Will Hutton/ Courtesy of the Penn State University Libraries; p. 157: © Jeff Greenberg/The Image Works; p. 169: © Mark Richards/PhotoEdit; p. 173: © Richard Pasley/Stock, Boston; p. 174: © 2002 Robert Daemmrich/Stone; p. 188: © David Young-Wolff/PhotoEdit; p. 191: © Michael Newman/PhotoEdit; p. 203: © David Young-Wolff/PhotoEdit; p. 213: © Michael Newman/PhotoEdit; p. 221: © Gregg Mancuso/Stock, Boston; p. 223: © Richard Pasley/Stock, Boston; p. 234: © Cleo Photography/PhotoEdit; p. 237: © Bonnie Kamin/PhotoEdit.

Printed in the U.S.A.

Library of Congress Control Number: 2001131478

ISBN: 0-618-06153-3

123456789-HWK-05 04 03 02 01

Contents

Introduction

You are about to come to a critical turning point in your life: the point where you discover that you can take charge of your life. Many amazing things will begin to happen. This course will show you how to take hold of your future and make it what you want it to be.

Your success depends to a large extent on two things: accepting *personal responsibility* for things that happen to you and making a *personal commitment* to accomplish your goals. *Navigating Your Future* emphasizes the importance of developing a sense of self-awareness—realizing you can take charge of your life—and setting life goals. Self-awareness and a commitment to achieving your goals are prerequisites for success.

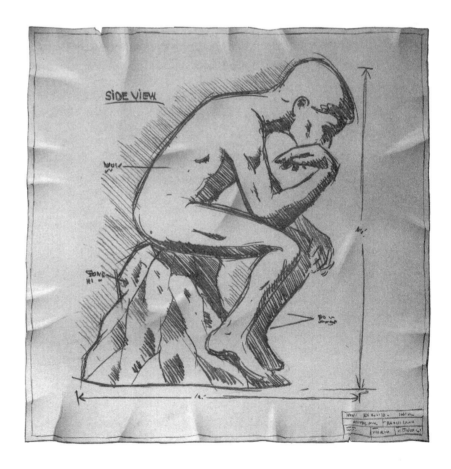

BLOOM'S TAXONOMY

The learning style utilized in this text is based on Bloom's taxonomy of educational objectives. Bloom's taxonomy defines six levels of learning, from lowest to highest: **knowledge, comprehension, application, analysis, synthesis,** and **evaluation.** These levels form a hierarchy in which each level demands the master of the lower-order learning skills (see the diagram printed on the inside front cover). As you move to higher levels in the hierarchy, your thinking abilities improve and you become capable of higher-level learning outcomes.

DEVELOPING CRITICAL THINKING SKILLS

By the time you reach the higher levels of Bloom's taxonomy, you are well on your way to becoming a critical thinker, which is one of the cornerstones of college success. *By developing your abilities as an active and collaborative learner, and by operating at all six levels of Bloom's taxonomy, you will be fully prepared to meet the rigors of college learning.* You will develop higher levels of thinking and enjoy success in your academic career and in the future.

ARRANGEMENT OF CHAPTERS

The chapters in this book are arranged to reflect a sequence of concerns that students typically encounter during their first semester of college. The course

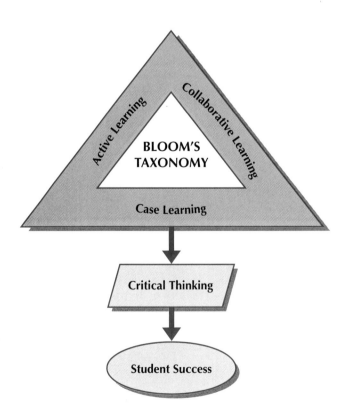

begins by dealing with the immediate problems of getting off to a good start. The next section covers college study skills such as note taking, test taking, and reading. The final section deals with long-run issues such as selecting a major and a career, developing a system of personal values, and preparing for lifelong success. Let's take a closer look at these sections of the course.

Getting Off to a Good Start The first section of this course is critical to the whole process and can be summed up in one word: goals. Setting effective goals is the best way to get off to a good start in college and it is the key to a successful college career and a successful life. The goal-setting process begins with a personal assessment of your strengths and weaknesses and an evaluation of your likes and dislikes. Once you set effective goals, you must make a *personal commitment* to accomplish them and determine the steps you need to take to reach them. About 20 percent of this course deals with the power of goals, your personal passageway to success.

Learning How to Develop Your Basic Skills The second section of this course is devoted to developing and sharpening your basic college learning skills. These skills are important because you will use them every day to accomplish your goals of earning a college degree and finding your first job. This section is placed near the beginning of the text so you can maximize its benefits throughout the semester. The sooner you master these skills, the sooner you will be fully equipped to achieve college success. Each chapter focuses on an important learning skill—time management, note taking, reading, test taking, writing, researching, and critical thinking.

Planning Your Future and Developing Your Personal Values The last section of this course focuses on exploring the long-range aspects of your life, developing your self-awareness, and developing your own set of personal values. As a first-year student, many views you currently hold are the product of your upbringing. In college, you have a chance to reaffirm old beliefs or develop new beliefs about important life issues such as drugs, alcohol, sex, diversity, and a host of other subjects. This is part of the personal responsibility of being an independent adult.

ORGANIZATION OF EACH CHAPTER

Each chapter of this course contains the following features to facilitate your learning and your instructor's teaching.

- *Chapter Objectives.* A clear, concise list of learning objectives highlights what you can expect to learn in the chapter.
- *Learning Exercises.* Throughout each chapter, learning exercises help you to become actively and collaboratively involved in your own learning by thinking about a topic or taking action. Some of these exercises deal with diversity, ethics, using the Internet, or personal responsibility. The collaborative learning exercises help strengthen your ability to work in teams and increase your mastery of the subject

matter. You will find out how groups often develop better solutions to problems than one person can alone. These subjects are covered in specific chapters, but they are important enough to be addressed throughout the entire course.

- *Chapter Highlights.* At the end of each chapter, a summary of the most important topics helps to reinforce your grasp of the key points.

- *Case Studies.* At the end of each chapter, a case study highlights a first-year college student who is facing a problem related to the material in the chapter. Studying these cases will help you apply the knowledge you gained in the chapter. The cases will also help you develop your collaborative learning and critical thinking skills.

- *Personal Journal.* Writing journal entries encourages you to reflect on what you have learned, how your intellectual positions have changed, and how you will relate what you have learned to your previous knowledge base.

- *Chapter Quiz.* At the end of each chapter, a series of short-essay questions covers the major points so you can test your retention of the material covered.

In summary, this course is organized to enhance your learning by putting theory into practice. *Navigating Your Future* does not just talk about the advantages of active learning, collaborative learning, and critical thinking skills; it utilizes all of these learning skills to help you discover the basics of student success.

▲ A Message from the Authors

Having spent many years teaching student success courses, the authors of this book have a genuine commitment to helping students succeed. How well your first semester goes has a great deal to do with whether you stick around for graduation. That is why the learning objective of this book is to help you succeed early in college. In addition, many of the skills taught in this course will prove invaluable to you long after you complete your degree.

This book is the result of teaching a freshman student success course for more than ten years at a major public research-oriented university. A great deal of the material (especially the case studies) is the product of our experiences with thousands of students who took that course. These experiences give us a unique perspective on student success because every day we help students make the transition to college learning and guide them through majors within a large university setting. We prepare them for careers in science, technology, or the traditional liberal arts, and then send some of them on to graduate school for their master's and doctoral degrees. Some go on to professional education in medical, dental, business, or law schools.

It is our desire that each one of you experience success, not only in college but in all aspects of your life. Have a successful future!

▲ *Valuable Classroom Resources*

1. *College Survival Consulting Services.* College Survival is the leading source of expertise, support services, and materials for student success courses. We are committed to promoting and supporting effective success courses within the higher education community.

   For more than fifteen years, Houghton Mifflin's College Survival consultants have provided consultation and training for the design, implementation, and presentation of student success and first-year courses. Our team of consultants have a wide variety of experience in teaching and administering the first-year course. They can provide help in establishing or improving your student success program. We offer assistance in course design, instructor training, teaching strategies, and much more. Contact us today at 1-800-528-8323, or visit us on the web at college.hmco.com.

2. *College Survival Web Site (college.hmco.com).* This web site offers new ways for students and teachers to learn. The *Navigating Your Future* web site includes quizzes, PowerPoint slides, and expanded work on the case studies found within the text.

3. *Instructor's Resource Manual.* The instructor's resource manual offers educators chapter-by-chapter suggestions for teaching, sample syllabi, an explanation of the text's pedagogy and references, and supplemental exercises and activities for each chapter.

4. *"Roundtable Discussions" Videotapes.* These two videotapes, "Study Strategies" and "Life Skills," feature five college students who discuss and seek solutions to the problems they face in college and in life. Call Faculty Services at 1-800-733-1717, visit the College Survival web site, or contact your Houghton Mifflin representative for more information. A teaching unit for the videotapes is also available on the College Survival web site.

5. *Myers-Briggs Type Indicator® (MBTI®) Instrument.* * This is the most widely used personality inventory in history—shrinkwrapped with *Navigating Your Future* for a discounted price at qualified schools. The standard form M self-scorable instrument contains 93 items that determine preferences on four scales: Extraversion-Introversion, Sensing-Intuition, Thinking-Feeling, and Judging-Perceiving.

   *MBTI and Myers-Briggs Type Indicator are registered trademarks of Consulting Psychologists Press, Inc.

6. *Retention Management System™ College Student Inventory.* The Noel Levitz College Student Inventory instrument is available in a specially priced package with this text. This early-alert, early-intervention program identifies students with tendencies that contribute to dropping out of school. Students can participate in an integrated, campus-wide program. Advisors are sent three interpretative reports: The Student's Report, the Advisor/Counselor Report, and

The College Summary and Planning Report. For more information, contact your College Survival consultant at 1-800-528-8323 or your local Houghton Mifflin Sales Representative.

7. *The College Survival Student Planner.* This week-at-a-glance academic planner is available in a specially priced package with this text. Produced in partnership with Premier, A Franklin Covey Company, The College Survival Student Planner assists students in managing their time both on and off campus. The planner includes a "Survival Kit" of helpful success tips from Houghton Mifflin Company College Survival textbooks.

▲ Acknowledgments

No project of this sort is ever possible without the support and guidance of many people. We would like to thank the more than ninety current and former teachers of our first-year seminar at The Pennsylvania State University who since 1987 have provided us with experiences and insights into what makes for student success. In particular, we would like to thank Felix Lukezic, James Levin, Ellen Taricani, Helen Smith, James Mortensen, and Edgar Yoder for their valuable comments, support, and counsel during the development of this book. We extend a special thanks to our families—Jean, Julie, and Jim Beierlein, and William, Laurie, and Amy Wade—allowing us to pursue projects such as book writing. At Houghton Mifflin we would like to thank Barbara Heinssen and her dedicated staff—Shani Fisher and Jonathan Wolfe. We wish to also thank Steve Mikels of Houghton Mifflin for his support throughout this project.

A number of reviewers have made valuable contributions to this book, and we would like to thank them for their guidance:

Peg Adams, Northern Kentucky University, KY

Michael D. Bird, Indiana University, IN

Karen Callender, City College of New York, NY

Dana Carpenter, Southern University and A&M College, LA

Barbara W. Chandler, St. Charles County Community College, MO

Leslie A. Chilton, Arizona State University, AZ

Judith Schein Cohen, University of Illinois at Chicago, IL

William Collins, University of Michigan, MI

Debra Grow, Pennsylvania State University, PA

David Johns, University of Delaware, DE

Alice Lanning, University of Oklahoma, OK

Judith A. Lynch, Kansas State University, KS

Joel V. McGee, Texas A&M University, TX

Karen W. Pool, Utah Valley State College, UT

Karen B. Quinn, University of Illinois at Chicago, IL

Elmo Slider, California State University–Sacramento, CA

Annette Toms, Syracuse University, NY

Steven M. Walsh, California State University, Bakersfield, CA

Virginia Weaver, University of Southern Maine, ME

Edward Wesley, St. Francis College, NY

Molly Widdicombe, University of Idaho, ID

JoAnn Yaworski, West Chester University, PA

J.G.B.

B.K.W.

CHAPTER 1

Understanding Who You Are and What You Want to Be

CHAPTER OBJECTIVES

After reading this chapter, you will understand why:

- Understanding who you are begins with developing self-awareness.
- College-level learning can help you decide what you want to be.
- Goals are important to your success.
- Having the proper attitude is important to your success.
- You belong in college.
- There is no such thing as a "typical" college student today.
- Keeping a personal journal is an important part of your personal growth.

After reading this chapter, you will know how to:

- Develop your sense of self-awareness.
- Take personal responsibility for your life.
- Make a personal commitment to your success.
- Understand your strengths and weaknesses.
- Use college-level learning to help you decide what you want to be.
- Use backward planning to help you decide what you want to be.
- Develop your plan for success.

Welcome to college! You finally made it. All those years of hard work and planning have paid off. Now you have a new goal: a college education. You are about to begin one of the greatest adventures of your life. By the time you graduate from college, you will be a different person than you are today. Obviously you will be a better-educated person, but you will also be able to think for yourself and embark on a lifetime of successful living.

Having lots of questions and a few self-doubts is quite normal in your first year of college, because everything is new and different. This is true whether you are 18 or 88. Remember, you would not be at this college if it did not expect you to graduate and succeed. Since you enrolled in this student success course, you are probably serious about your future and determined to learn how to succeed in college. This course will help you achieve that goal.

Success begins with understanding who you are and what you want to be. You started that process very early in life. Back then it was easy, since other people (usually parents, teachers, coaches, community leaders) told you who you were and what you ought to be. They often made decisions for you, such as what classes you took, what clothes you wore, what activities you participated in, and who your friends were. Now that you are older, you have to make these decisions for yourself and take responsibility for your own life.

This is a journey without end because you will always be learning new things about yourself, sometimes redefining what you want to be. How successful you are in life depends on your level of commitment to the goals you set. When your commitment is high, your rewards will be high. Success is mostly a personal matter—a matter of *personal responsibility* and *personal commitment*. If you take the exercises in each chapter seriously, you will increase your understanding of who you are and what drives you to succeed. You will also have a better idea of what you want from life and how to accomplish it. It is all up to you.

▲ *Understanding Who You Are Begins with Self-Awareness*

Understanding who you are begins with developing a sense of self-awareness. **Self-awareness** is the ability to stand apart from yourself, see yourself from afar, and think objectively about yourself. It is as though you step out of your body and see yourself as others see you. As your sense of self-awareness grows, you will realize that you are able to do more than just react instinctively to the things around you. You will realize that you do not have to let outside forces control

your life; rather, you can take control of your own life. You can anticipate, analyze, and prepare for events. You can learn from your past mistakes and the mistakes of others. Self-awareness is the first step in understanding who you are and what you want to be.

Although you can learn from others, you also need to analyze, re-analyze, and question what you do. An old story about a family at dinnertime illustrates this point well. The father went into the kitchen to see how the family's dinner was coming. As he entered, he saw his daughter cut off about a third of a beautiful boneless ham and throw it in the garbage before putting the rest of it into the oven. When he asked her why she did that, she responded that this was how her mother had taught her to cook a ham. He went into the living room and asked his wife if that was the right way to prepare a ham. She said it was—in fact, it was how *her* mother had taught her to do it. Then he asked his mother-in-law, who agreed with his wife. She assured him that this was as much ham as she could fit into the tiny oven she had when she was first married many years ago.

This story reminds us that although some decisions made sense yesterday, they may be wrong today or tomorrow. In this story, the family had thrown away countless pounds of good ham for years because no one thought about *why* they were doing it. What had been a good decision when the mother-in-law was first married was no longer appropriate. The daughter could have easily cooked the whole ham in her bigger, more modern oven. When she threw away a third of the ham, she had made a conscious decision to let past conditions control her. She had decided not to think about what she was doing but to continue to do as she had always done. Her decision was her choice, not something that was beyond her control. To break with family tradition and bake the whole ham, she would have to (1) take the initiative to make a decision and (2) assume personal responsibility for it if the decision turns out to be a bad one (i.e., results in wasted meat). On the other hand, if all goes well (everybody wants second helpings), she has found a great way to increase the amount of ham available.

TAKING PERSONAL RESPONSIBILITY FOR YOUR LIFE

Increasing your self-awareness and making decisions for yourself can be very exciting whether you are cooking a ham or going to school. You can choose to have your conditions control you, or you can choose to take charge of your life. For many students, college is their first chance to exercise some control over their lives. You can choose to skip class, arrive late for work, or sleep until noon, and nobody can do anything about it. But decision making also carries the risk that your decision will be the wrong one.

Making sound decisions means being mature enough to take personal responsibility for their consequences. For example, if you skip class and fail to make up the material covered that day, you may receive a lower grade in the course. Your lower grade will be the direct result of your decision to skip class. You must take personal responsibility for that decision because it was your choice and not something beyond your control.

You can see why some people prefer others to make their decisions for them. Not only is it easier and safer, but it never seems to be their fault when something goes wrong. They do not have to take any risks or suffer any consequences—in fact, they do not even have to think. At this point, you might ask: Then why should I waste my time or take the risks of making my own decisions? The answer is that if you do not make your own decisions, you will always get what someone else wants for you. This is usually much less satisfying than getting what *you* want.

Making your own decisions means you have to know what you want. Consider Alice in *Through the Looking Glass*. She comes to a fork in the road and asks the Cheshire Cat which way to go. He asks her where she is going, and she replies that she does not know. He tells her that it therefore doesn't matter which road she takes.

You have to know where you want to go before you can make good decisions. Success and happiness come to those who are willing to take the initiative to make decisions and do the things that bring about personal success. Your choice to attend college required you to exercise your initiative and make a decision. Now it is time for you to take personal responsibility for your decision by doing all you can to make your college experience a success.

MAKING A PERSONAL COMMITMENT TO YOUR SUCCESS

Aspiring to a better life and working to become a better student are important first steps on the road to success. Unfortunately, by themselves they are not enough. You must have a personal commitment to these ideas, meaning you are willing to give them high priority in your life and do what it takes to accomplish them. It may mean making many short-run sacrifices to achieve these **long-run goals**. It may mean giving up a weekend at the beach to finish a term paper or study for a test. What you are willing to give up to achieve your long-run goals is a measure of your personal commitment to them. It is your personal commitment to your goals that makes the difference between success and failure.

Exercise 1.1 *Think about a situation where you made a good decision. On a separate sheet of paper, write one or two paragraphs describing the situation and your choices. Explain why you made your decision and why you think it was a good one. Describe how you felt about your decision when you first made it. How did you feel after it turned out to be a good choice? Discuss at least two things you learned from this decision that could help you make more good decisions in the future.*

Exercise 1.2 *Think about a situation where you made a bad decision. On a separate sheet of paper, write one or two paragraphs describing the situation and your choices. Explain why you made your decision and why you think it was a bad one. Describe how you felt about your decision when you first made it. How did you feel after it turned out to be a bad choice? Discuss at least two things you learned from this decision that could help you make better decisions in the future.*

Exercise 1.3 *On a separate sheet of paper, write one or two paragraphs that cover the following:*

1. Describe the best job and the worst job you ever had. What were the best aspects of each job? What were the worst aspects? What did you learn about yourself from your two very different job experiences?
2. Describe the ideal job for you. What would be the worst job for you?

Exercise 1.4 *Assume you have made a total commitment to achieving success in college. Describe at least one aspect of college that is interfering right now with your personal commitment to success. Then describe what you need to do to eliminate this problem.*

_____

_____

_____

_____

_____

▲ *Understanding What You Want to Be Begins with College-Level Learning*

One of the most common statements made by beginning college students is "I don't know what I want to do with my life. Maybe I should take a year off from school and try to figure it out." This is unfortunate since college, especially courses like this one, is a great place to find answers to this dilemma. A 1999 U.S. Department of Education study found that only 23 percent of students who dropped out of college for a year or more ended up getting their degree before age 30. On the other hand, 70 percent of those who stayed in school eventually got their degree. The value of staying in school can also be measured by income level. The study showed that in 1998, college graduates between ages 24 and 34 earned $14,000 more annually than individuals without a college degree.

College is where most people learn to think for themselves. Few places offer a more challenging environment or are more likely to transform your life. Your mind will be opened, expanded, and exposed to more new ideas during your college years than at any other time in your life. More important, you will develop the skills you need to begin a lifetime of learning. Most people have fond memories of their college experience because it represents a major transition in the way they think and in how they live their lives.

If you are skeptical of these claims, that is a good sign. It means you are learning to think for yourself. Most students enter college with limited views and a short list of potential careers. By the time you graduate, you will be thinking for yourself and possibly headed for a career in a field you never dreamed of before coming to college. You might pursue a field you know little about right now, such as acoustics, rural sociology, bioengineering, linguistics, or business logistics.

Your enrollment in this course means you have made a personal commitment to success and are eager to find out what you want to do with your life. It is perfectly acceptable to admit that you do not have all the answers. The important thing is that *you* decide what those answers will be. It may take a while to decide what you want to do with your life, and you may change your mind several times along the way. What you want to avoid is ending up like the person whose medical school diploma hangs in the lobby of the restaurant he now owns and manages. His parents told him he could do anything he wanted to with his life *after* he graduated from medical school!

UNDERSTANDING YOUR STRENGTHS AND WEAKNESSES

Determining what you want to be starts with a thorough self-examination of your strengths and weaknesses. The next four active learning exercises provide ways for you to do this. Like all the exercises in this book, this one is not a test, and there are no right or wrong answers. You need only answer the questions completely and honestly.

ACTIVE LEARNING

Exercise 1.5 *Take the self-assessment exercise of your strengths and weaknesses found at this web site:*

http://www.adm.uwaterloo.ca/infocecs/CRC/docs/self-assess.html

Exercise 1.6 *Take some of the self-assessment exercises provided at this web site:*

http://www.bgsu.edu/offices/student_affairs/career/univ/index.html

Exercise 1.7 *After completing Exercises 1.5 and 1.6, write one or two paragraphs on a separate sheet of paper that answer the following questions:*

1. What specific things did you learn about yourself for the first time?

2. Based on what you learned, would you modify what you want to do with your life? If so, how?

3. What else do you want to learn about yourself that these assessments didn't cover?

Exercise 1.8 *After completing Exercises 1.5 and 1.6, describe, in one or two paragraphs, which of your personal strengths will enhance your career. Which ones will improve your relationships? Which ones will enhance your school's reputation?*

THE ROLE OF COLLEGE-LEVEL LEARNING

College-level learning requires you to think about yourself in terms of what is important and not important to you, what you like and do not like, and what you do well and not so well. As you increase your self-awareness and gain a better understanding of your strengths and weaknesses, you will develop a better sense of what you want to do with your life.

Actor Tommy Lee Jones described his motivation for obtaining his Harvard University liberal arts degree: "Knowledge allows you to make informed decisions

as you make your way through this vale of tears. Ignorance is the huge enemy. The more we know, the better we think, the less fearful and the better life gets" (*Parade*, June 6, 1997, p. 5).

Exercise 1.9 *How does Tommy Lee Jones's affiliation with Harvard University strengthen his voice on the subjects of knowledge, thinking, and life? Explain your own positions on these subjects. Do you think your voice is more credible than Jones's, less credible, or equally credible? Why?*

_____

_____

_____

_____

_____

BACKWARD PLANNING

Once you have developed an understanding of who you are and assessed your strengths and weaknesses, the next step is to decide what you want to be. You can determine this by using backward planning. Backward planning means thinking about what the final product (you) should look like someday and then working backward to decide what you must do to generate the desired outcome. Backward planning enables you to see what skills, accomplishments, and experiences you need today to reach the life you see yourself in tomorrow.

Backward planning is a good way to determine your life goals. By first finding out what you want to accomplish during your lifetime, you should then be able to determine what you value most and what you need to do now to make it happen. In other words, once you see the big picture of your life, you can confidently work on the smaller sections.

Exercises 1.10 and 1.11 will help you identify your life goals for the next ten years and for the time you reach retirement age. Exercise 1.12 will help you rank your accomplishments so you can decide which ones are most important to you and deserve your personal commitment. If you have already thought this through, these exercises will reconfirm your ideas. If you have never done this before and have no definitive life goals, this is your chance to decide what you want to do with your life. Remember to use what you learned about yourself in Exercises 1.5 through 1.8 to help you come up with your answers. Although your answers may start out vague, at least you will have put something down. You can always change your answers later. The objective is to get you thinking about your life and what you want out of it.

Exercise 1.10 *Pretend that it is ten years from now. Write your résumé by filling in as much information as you can for each of the following headings. You will have to use your imagination, envisioning yourself in a career course ideal for you.*

Employment Objective:

_____

_____

_____

Past Experience:

_____

_____

_____

Current Job Title:

_____

_____

_____

Summary of Duties and Responsibilities:

_____

_____

_____

Education:

_____

_____

_____

Technical Skills:

_____

_____

_____

Oral and Communication Skills:

_____

_____

_____

Professional Accomplishments:

_____

_____

_____

Community Service:

_____

_____

_____

ACTIVE LEARNING

Exercise 1.11 _Assume you are now 80 years old and preparing for retirement after a long and successful career. The following people have been invited to a dinner in your honor and asked to say a few words to sum up your life from their perspective. What would you like each of them to say about you?_

Spouse:

_____

_____

_____

Children:

_____

_____

Friends:

_____

_____

Coworkers:

_____

_____

Religious Leaders:

_____

_____

Community Leaders:

_____

_____

_____

Exercise 1.12 _On a separate piece of paper, draw a time line of your life from birth to the end of your life (assume you live to be 100 years old!). Identify the key elements and accomplishments of your life and at what age they happened._

Exercise 1.13 *In Exercises 1.5 through 1.8, you discovered some things about your-self, including your strengths and weaknesses.*

1. Rank those items from most to least important to you. Then explain why you ranked the first three items as most important, and discuss what you are doing to enhance them.

_____

_____

_____

2. Explain why you ranked the last three items as least important.

_____

_____

_____

3. In what ways are you pleased with your rankings? Do any of them surprise you? If so, how?

_____

_____

_____

4. Do you see potential conflicts between any of these items? Explain.

_____

_____

_____

5. What do these rankings tell you about what you want out of life?

_____

_____

_____

▲ *The Power of Goals*

The items you ranked as most important in Exercise 1.13 are called life goals. **Life goals** are the major things in your life, things that you find very important to accomplish or fulfill. Achieving them is one way you will measure success in your life. The actions that will help you achieve your life goals deserve your strongest personal commitment.

Life goals begin as ideas or values, but they point the way to life accomplishments and careers. Goals will keep you focused on the things that are most important to you. People with written, clearly defined goals get more done and have more fulfilled lives. They are more satisfied because they have taken control of their lives. They see the progress they are making toward the accomplishment of the things that are most important to them.

The process of achieving life goals begins when you set basic life objectives. For example, suppose your life goal is to be a famous neurosurgeon. In this case, one of your first objectives would be to get good enough grades in college to be admitted to medical school. After completing medical school, you might accomplish things that help build your reputation as a neurosurgeon, such as developing a surgical procedure that saves many lives.

If your life goal is to be a research director for a major food company, you may need to assemble a bundle of goals. Your objectives might include a Ph.D. in nutrition, 10 to 15 years of experience in research and development with a large food company, training in business management, development of good written and oral communication skills, and the ability to work well in team environments. These objectives cannot be met simultaneously, but they can be accomplished sequentially over a lifetime career.

IT IS NEVER TOO EARLY TO HAVE GOALS

You may be thinking: I am just beginning college. Why do I have to worry about lifetime accomplishments right now? Most people's life goals take many years to accomplish. Longer-run life goals are more manageable when you break them down into **intermediate-run objectives** and **short-run objectives**. Unlike goals, **objectives** can be achieved one step at a time, such as graduating from college, passing the bar exam, or graduating from medical school.

For example, if obtaining a college degree is your intermediate-run objective (something you want to accomplish in the next five years), one of your short-run objectives (something you want to accomplish in the next six months to a year) would be to earn good grades. Another short-run objective would be to find a faculty adviser who can give you good career advice, help you with course scheduling, and make recommendations for a job, an internship, or graduate school. Progressing toward your life goals starts in the first semester of college and builds day by day, week by week, course by course, and semester by semester. It is never too early to start working on your life goals.

BLOOM'S AFFECTIVE DOMAIN AND YOUR GOALS

Besides the elements of Bloom's taxonomy for the cognitive domain described in the preface, Benjamin Bloom developed a taxonomy, or classification system, for the affective domain. The **affective domain** measures students' emotional maturity by classifying their attitudes, interests, appreciation, and modes of adjustment to particular phenomena or stimuli. This second taxonomy is as powerful as the first because your emotional maturity affects how you perform when confronted by a new situation such as college learning. In the context of this course, your level in the affective domain hierarchy has a great deal to do with your level of commitment to achieving your life goals and your chances for college success.

The taxonomy of the affective domain is organized in the same way as the taxonomy of the cognitive domain. Five levels of attitudes are identified in a hierarchy in which each higher-order classification demands the mastery of lower-order skills and abilities (see Figure 1.1). The five levels, from lowest to highest, are **receiving**, **responding**, **valuing**, **organization**, and **characterization by a value or value complex**. As you move to higher levels in the hierarchy, your level of emotional maturity increases. You are more likely to have a realistic sense of self-awareness, a reachable set of life goals, and a clearer view of the world and how it works.

Robert Linn and Norman Gronlund, well-known educational psychologists, summarized the meaning of each of these five levels in the affective domain and the associated educational outcomes as follows:

1. *Receiving*

   Gives attention to learning.

   Students show this level of attitude toward learning by listening attentively, being aware of the value of learning, and attending to classroom activities.

2. *Responding*

   Actively participates or reacts to learning.

   Students show this level of attitude toward learning by completing assignments, following class policies and procedures, participating in classroom activities, volunteering for classroom tasks, displaying their interest in the subject, and cheerfully helping classmates with schoolwork.

3. *Valuing*

   Gives value to learning.

   Students demonstrate this level of attitude toward learning by showing their appreciation for all learning, exhibiting a concern for the welfare of others, demonstrating a positive attitude toward problem solving, and displaying a commitment to social and personal improvement.

4. *Organization*

   Synthesizes and compares different values, and begins building an internally consistent personal value system.

   Students show this level of attitude toward learning by indicating that they recognize the need for

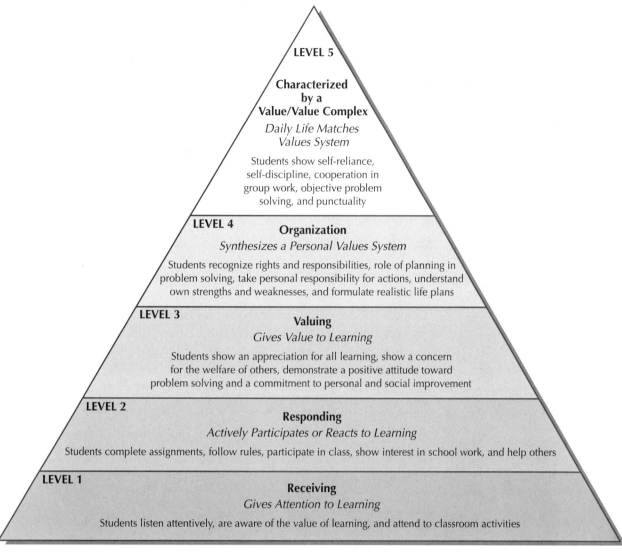

FIGURE 1.1 Bloom's Taxonomy of the Affective Domain

balance between rights and responsibilities in a democracy; they recognize the role of systematic planning in problem solving; they accept responsibility for personal behavior; and they understand their personal strengths and weaknesses, formulating a life plan in harmony with their abilities, interests, and beliefs.

5. *Characterization by a value or value complex* **Exhibits a behavior reflecting daily adherence to a lifestyle that follows the value system developed at the organization level of the hierarchy.**

Students show this level of attitude toward learning by demonstrating consciousness of safety, self-reliance, cooperation in group activities, and an objective approach to problem solving; they demonstrate industry, punctuality, self-discipline, and good health habits.

Educator John Dewey once described the attitudes needed for correct thinking as *open-mindedness, wholeheartedness,* and *responsibility.* He argued that "Knowledge of methods alone will not suffice; there must be the desire, the will to employ them" (Dewey, p. 30). Without achieving a higher level of emotional maturity in the affective domain, individuals cannot arrive at sound conclusions. Your attitude is a vital part of your personal commitment to defining and achieving your life goals.

LIFE GOALS CAN BE CHANGED

Just because you select a life goal today does not mean you are stuck with it forever. You can always change it later. When asked how they got to where they are today, many successful people respond something like this: "It's an interesting story. I started out to be a . . . , but then this happened and things changed." New goals may make you aware of new opportunities. New information may change your life goals as you continually explore what life has to offer. Exercise 1.14 is designed to help you translate your life goals into shorter-run objectives so you can start working toward them today.

Exercise 1.14 *Describe the life goals you identified in Exercise 1.13. What short-run objectives for this semester will help you accomplish these goals? List specific things you will do this semester to accomplish your short-run objectives. What do you need to do this month to realize those objectives? What do you need to do this week to accomplish them? What do you need to do today to achieve them?*

_____

_____

_____

_____

_____

ETHICS

Exercise 1.15 *Describe who can choose or alter your life goals. Justify your answer.*

_____

_____

_____

_____

_____

▲ What This Means for You

This chapter has introduced you to many critical issues. The material presented is probably difficult to master, especially in your first semester. You will realize the benefits of this chapter when you take what it presents seriously and look at your responses as a first draft of your life plan. You may come up with many more drafts throughout your life, but if you do this right, you will never get to the final copy. That will be left to those who write your obituary.

We have all known people who had their futures all figured out in the fourth grade. The girl who sat across from you was going to be a nuclear physicist, a doctor, or a CPA. There was never any question about it. For most of us, however, developing a sense of self-awareness and deciding what we want to do with our lives is a long, demanding process, often with many false starts. What matters is not how often you fail or change your mind but what you learn and how it makes the next version of your life plan even better. Many very successful people encounter problems along the way, but they view them as temporary setbacks on the road to success rather than as permanent roadblocks. Their life goals and objectives, their personal commitment to their success, and their willingness to take personal responsibility for what happens are what set them apart from less successful people. As you use the tools presented in this chapter, you too will develop important skills for success.

▲ Why You Belong in College

The world of today requires greater thinking skills than that of the past. Learning is a lifelong activity, and college is one of the best places to continue to develop the thinking skills you need for success.

As you look around your classroom and your campus, you will most likely see a wide assortment of people. Prior to World War II, college was only for a select few. Most college students were male, ranged in age from 18 to 22 years, came from wealthy families, attended college full-time, and received a baccalaureate degree that marked the end of their education. Most jobs did not require a college degree. None of these things are true anymore.

The "typical student" no longer exists. Today's colleges have students of nearly every age, socioeconomic level, ethnic background, and marital status. Some students are new high school graduates; others have returned to college after many years in the work force. The latter group is often the one with the clearest life goals and the greatest motivation to succeed in college. Some students attend while supporting families, and others attend part-time at night. Many students commute long distances to take their courses. All of these individuals are regular components of today's "typical college student profile." What connects them all is a common desire for a better, more rewarding life as they learn to think for themselves.

CHAPTER HIGHLIGHTS

1. Being an adult means making decisions for yourself and taking responsibility for your life. This includes deciding who you are and what you want to be. You can control your reactions to the world around you.

2. Understanding who you are begins with developing your self-awareness.

3. Self-awareness is the ability to see yourself from afar and think objectively about yourself and what you do. It is like stepping out of your body and seeing yourself as others see you. Self-awareness is a distinctly human trait and allows you to plan your future.

4. You can learn from others, but you also need to analyze, re-analyze, and question what you do. You do this because you can control what happens in your life.

5. Making your own decisions also means being mature enough to take personal responsibility for the consequences of your decisions.

6. Many people are interested in success, but few are personally committed to success.

7. College is where many people learn to think for themselves. Therefore, college is a great place to decide what you want to be and what you want to do with your life.

8. A college education can equip you to begin a lifetime of learning.

9. Goals help you focus on what is important to you.

10. A personal journal is a wonderful way to measure your growth and increasing self-awareness.

CHAPTER HIGHLIGHTS

CASE STUDY
Angela's Angst

It was just after 11:00 P.M. when Julie opened the door to her dorm room and turned on the light. She was surprised to find Angela, her roommate, sitting in the dark. Julie knew Angela seemed down the last couple of days. Both of them had recently struggled with their first round of semester tests, but Angela had taken her mediocre grades very hard. Julie had tried to tell her they were not that bad for a first-semester student. But Angela kept saying, "What will my parents say when they see these horrible grades? I know I have disappointed them. I'll never get into a good law school now. What am I going to do?"

As Julie tried to console her roommate, she thought about what Angela had told her about her background in the few weeks they had lived together. Angela is the oldest of three children and the first member of her family to attend college. Her two younger brothers will follow her to college and major in engineering. Her father made that very clear when her parents moved Angela into the dorm. In the first week of the semester Julie sensed that Angela was really enjoying college, but as time went on Angela's enjoyment seemed to come more from the relief of being on her own.

During high school, Angela's mother got her up at 6:00 A.M. so Angela could practice the piano for an hour before school. Her parents expected her to come home directly after school to keep an eye on her brothers, except on days when she had marching band practice. Angela once confided to Julie that she always did what her parents told her to do. She even voted for their favorite candidate in the last presidential election.

College was nothing like Angela thought it would be. She had trouble seeing how Introduction to Political Science could lead her to a good law school, despite what her mother had told her. In fact, she had come to this school because of the reputation of its political science program. Her father said it was one of the best in the country.

As Angela began to open up that night, she told Julie what was making her feel so depressed. Political science class that day was about the death penalty. When her professor found out that she wanted to be a lawyer, he asked her a difficult question: If she were a prosecuting attorney, could she recommend that someone be put to death? Angela was not sure she could do that. It was then that the whole idea of becoming a lawyer began to feel like a bad decision. It had always been her parents' dream to have a lawyer in the family. She had trouble seeing herself in college for another seven years. As she began to search her soul, she was not sure she even wanted to be in college. The idea of becoming a lawyer began to fade, and Angela realized that she really had no idea what she wanted to do with her life.

Angela looked at Julie and asked her what she thought she should do.

If you were Julie, what would you say to Angela?

Personal Journal

One of the best ways to increase your self-awareness is to put your thoughts down on paper. At the end of each chapter, you will be asked to make entries in your personal journal. For this chapter, your personal journal assignment will cover what you learned about yourself from all the chapter exercises.

Writing in a journal forces you to think clearly. You can reflect on what you have written, revise it, make its meaning clearer, and put your thoughts in a more logical sequence. The journal's most enduring value is that it measures your personal growth. Since it is written, you can save it and look at it in the future. Reread your journal entries at the end of the semester and at the end of the school year. As you approach graduation, look at them again. Most students are amazed at the changes they see in themselves: how they think and how they live their lives.

SELF-AWARENESS

Personal Journal Exercise 1.1 Reflect on the material covered in this chapter and on what you have learned. Then write a paragraph or two in your journal answering the following questions: (1) Describe a typical day at college for you. Has college been what you expected? What has surprised you the most about college so far? What has surprised you the least? (2) What do you like best about college? What do you like least? (3) Describe your life goals and explain why you chose them. (4) How have you changed since you entered college? How has your life changed?

_____

_____

_____

_____

_____

DIVERSITY

Personal Journal Exercise 1.2 Write a paragraph or two answering the following questions: (1) Describe the "typical college student" at your school (or explain why there is no "typical" student at your school). (2) What do you think a "typical professor" is like at your school? (3) Discuss the diversity of students and faculty at your school. How do the people you have met at college compare to those you have known previously? (4) Describe the most interesting person you have met since coming to college. What makes this person interesting to you?

_____

_____

CHAPTER QUIZ

1. Explain why a sense of self-awareness is an important prerequisite to understanding who you are.

_____

_____

_____

_____

_____

2. How does backward planning help you decide what you want to be?

_____

_____

_____

_____

_____

3. What is the role of personal responsibility in making decisions for yourself?

_____

_____

_____

_____

_____

4. Why is college a great place to decide what you want to be?

_____

_____

_____

_____

_____

5. What is the relationship among life goals, objectives, intermediate-run objectives, and short-run objectives?

_____

_____

_____

_____

_____

ADDITIONAL RESOURCES

Canfield, Jack, and Mark Victor Hansen. _Chicken Soup for the Soul: 101 Stories to Open the Heart and Rekindle the Spirit._ Deerfield Beach, FL: Health Communications, Inc., 1993.

Covey, Stephen R. _The Seven Habits of Very Effective People: Restoring the Character Ethic._ New York: Simon & Schuster, 1989.

Covey, Stephen R., A. Roger Merrill, and Rebecca R. Merrill. _First Things First: To Live, to Love, to Learn, to Leave a Legacy._ New York: Simon & Schuster, 1994.

Dewey, John. _How We Think: A Restatement of the Relation of Reflective Thinking to the Educative Process,_ 2d ed. Lexington, MA: D.C. Heath, 1960.

Lakein, Alan. _How to Get Control of Your Time and Your Life._ New York: Signet Division of Penguin Books, 1974.

Linn, Robert L., and Norman E. Gronlund. _Measurement and Evaluation in Teaching,_ 8th ed. New York: Macmillan, 2000.

CHAPTER 2

Understanding Why You Came to College

CHAPTER OBJECTIVES

After reading this chapter, you will understand why:

- College can play a key role in reaching your life goals.
- Higher-level thinking skills (as defined in Bloom's taxonomy) are important to being a critical thinker.
- Being a critical thinker prepares you for college success.
- A college education prepares you for lifelong learning.
- Education is different from training.
- Education should make you feel uncomfortable.
- A liberal arts education has value for your life and education.

After reading this chapter, you will know how to:

- Determine your level of commitment to your college education.
- Use college to reach your life goals.
- Make education a lifetime activity.
- Apply Bloom's taxonomy to enhance your learning.

In the last chapter, you began your journey to success by understanding who you are and what you want to be. The self-discovery exercises you completed in that chapter were designed to get you to think objectively about what you are today, what you want to be tomorrow, and what you want out of your life. These are vital issues that everyone needs to think about often throughout his or her lifetime.

In this chapter, you will ask yourself another important question: Why did I come to college? You will begin to answer that question by looking at why many people believe college plays a significant role in accomplishing their life goals. At the end of the chapter, you will develop your own reasons for being in college. What matters is that *you* know why you came to college and that you know exactly what *you* want to get from it. This knowledge will strengthen your personal commitment to success in college and in life.

▲ The Role of College in Reaching Your Life Goals

For most of you, reaching your life goals means you must acquire new skills and develop new talents beyond those you already possess. In the past, even with no education beyond high school, people who were bright and worked hard had many career opportunities. Today's world is very different. Fewer jobs require just a high school diploma, and many of those jobs are being automated out of existence or moved overseas. The remaining jobs normally pay little above minimum wage. Your ability to move above entry-level jobs depends to a great extent on acquiring skills and talents beyond those obtained in high school. Without these new abilities, you will be left behind.

EDUCATION AS A LIFELONG ACTIVITY

Not too long ago, a college education lasted a lifetime, standing the test of time and changing careers. Today technical skills that were first-rate at graduation are obsolete in a few years. Few occupations stand still; most are constantly adjusting to the technological changes in our world. Lifelong learning is now the new constant in our lives. Education has become like breathing: You need to do it every day to stay alive.

How can you successfully cope with these changes? One way is to get a good education and keep adding to it throughout your life. This will ensure that you will be in demand because you always have the skills employers want. You can also lay a good foundation for your post–high school education by learning the principles of critical thinking and problem solving. These principles adapt well to a changing technology and a changing work force. They are some of the most important skills you can master in your college education. Nearly all of your college courses, from math to literature, will demand critical thinking and problem solving. This advanced mode of thinking will take you from memorization to critical thinking and from passive learning to active learning. Such college-level learning will be a key element in your success.

College offers the best place to "load up" on the latest skills you need to be competitive in the job market. The principles of critical thinking and problem solving learned in college also give you the tools to efficiently carry out life-long learning. Thus, when you periodically return to college to "reload" with the latest knowledge and technical skills, you can do so efficiently. Through this lifelong process of educational renewal, you keep your skills current and your career moving forward.

LEARNING IN ELEMENTARY AND HIGH SCHOOL

You began your elementary education by focusing heavily on the basic skills of reading, writing, and arithmetic. These are the primary building blocks of learning and social interaction. You memorized the basics such as multiplication tables, spelling, grammar rules, and the fundamental laws of science. There is little argument that the product of 5 and 9 is 45.

The development of these basic skills was an important first step in nurturing your ability to learn. However, memorizing facts and basics will not be enough to keep you competitive in today's knowledge-intensive, rapidly evolving world.

THE NEED FOR HIGHER-LEVEL LEARNING SKILLS

If you began college immediately after graduating from high school, your family may have pressured you to attend college. You may have vaguely accepted their contention that higher education will be worth the effort and make your life better. If you entered the work force right after high school graduation, the frustration of trying to get ahead without a higher education is likely what brought you to college now.

No matter what brought you to this point, you will most likely realize very soon the power of independent thinking and other higher-level skills. You can obtain these skills in many ways, but typically the most efficient way is through a formal education that leads to a college degree. Some important things to

remember are that (1) knowledge is power, (2) technical knowledge quickly becomes obsolete, (3) lifelong learning is the only way to keep your skills current, and (4) the principles of critical thinking and problem solving are important prerequisites to lifelong learning.

One of the main purposes of this course is to transform you into a critical thinker. A **critical thinker** is ready for the rigors of college and lifelong learning because he or she can

1. Distinguish between facts and opinions

2. Draw valid conclusions from data

3. Recognize the assumptions underlying conclusions

4. Recognize the limitations of data

5. Integrate learning from different areas into a plan for solving a problem

6. Clearly explain concepts orally or in writing to others

To be a critical thinker, you must be able to think at the highest levels of **Bloom's taxonomy of the cognitive domain**. (See the inside cover of this text for a full discussion of Bloom's taxonomy.) The remaining chapter exercises and case studies will help you develop these higher-level thinking skills. Developing these skills early in your college career will increase your ability to do well in college and in life.

▲ *Education Versus Training*

One long-standing argument among students and educators is the difference between education and training. Both are important elements of our lifelong educational process, and both have an important place in our lives and in our society. It is important, though, to understand the difference between them so you will better understand the role of a college education in achieving your life goals.

Training focuses on having students remember, understand, and apply what they learn. Typically, it involves thinking at the first three levels of Bloom's taxonomy of the cognitive domain: knowledge, comprehension, and application. A good example is cardiopulmonary resuscitation (CPR) training as given in a first aid course. In terms of Bloom's taxonomy, the desired educational objectives for students in this training would include the following:

- *Remembering* what they have learned as demonstrated in their ability to recite major terms, definitions, and facts related to successfully administering CPR

- *Understanding* what they have learned as demonstrated in their ability to explain and paraphrase the CPR procedure they were taught

- *Applying* what they have learned as demonstrated in their ability to properly administer CPR

Education is more than training, that is, more than knowing what to do and demonstrating how to do it. An education covers all six levels of Bloom's taxonomy: knowledge, comprehension, application, analysis, synthesis, and evaluation. An education enables you to understand the reasons and principles behind "the what" and "the how" of doing something.

In terms of Bloom's taxonomy, the desired educational objectives for students enrolled in a CPR course at a medical school would differ from those offered as a first aid course to the general public. The educational objectives in the medical school course would include the first three educational objectives found in the training program. However, the objectives would go further to include the following three objectives found at the top of Bloom's taxonomy:

- *Recognizing* the unstated assumptions behind what was taught (as shown by the ability to see, for example, why CPR is administered differently to small children than to adults)

- *Integrating* the CPR training with what is taught in other medical school courses (for example, the ability to treat a patient with multiple injuries)

- *Evaluating* the procedure to find better ways to perform CPR (because of their deeper understanding of it, the medical students would not only know how to properly perform CPR but would also have the capacity to participate in formulating better CPR procedures and approaches)

For some things, an education may provide more than you want or need to know. If all you want to do is be able to administer CPR in a personal emergency, then CPR training is all you need. However, if you want to be an emergency room physician or to do cardiology research, you will need to have more than basic CPR training. An education ensures that you will be a full participant in your field and that you will be prepared to sharpen your skills throughout your career.

EDUCATION SHOULD MAKE YOU FEEL UNCOMFORTABLE

Getting an education is no easy feat. It often takes a lifetime to obtain the education you want, and you may feel uncomfortable along the way. However, forcing you out of your comfort zone is what an education is all about. If you do feel uncomfortable, it is because you are doing things that are new or different from what you normally do. Feeling uncomfortable means you are learning and growing. The pride of accomplishment you feel when you master something new more than compensates for any discomfort you experience while you are learning.

Each year you are in school, the size of your world and the level of your skills expand as you master increasingly difficult subjects. This is often a painful process. You may wrestle with certain subjects in school, and there is no guarantee that your learning struggles will end when you graduate from college. At that point, keeping your knowledge up to date is more important than ever. Since few people can return to school on a full-time basis every year or two, you will want to discover how to learn independently. A college education can equip you with the skills to continue your education long after you receive your diploma. In summary, being forced out of your comfort zone is a sign of progress and means you are continuing to learn.

▲ The Role of the Liberal Arts

A college education brings many responsibilities that come with being an educated person and a leader in society. Being a responsible citizen in a democracy demands more of you than just your technical know-how. You need to make wise decisions when you vote for candidates, vote on public issues, and serve on a jury. You also need to interact with others and solve the problems of everyday life.

The principles of critical thinking that you learn in college are equally valuable when you apply them to your personal and public lives. Thinking critically becomes easier when you understand the context of a problem and what has occurred in the past. That is why it is important for you to study history, art, political science, and other basic subjects. Good problem solving requires the ability to analyze, synthesize, and evaluate many aspects of a problem to reach a wise decision. This wide collection of knowledge is called the *liberal arts*.

Nearly every college incorporates the liberal arts into its curriculum as a set of general education requirements taken by all students. This broad set of courses ensures that you can appreciate the many aspects of human existence and that you are properly prepared to be a responsible citizen and leader. These courses foster a love of lifetime learning and educate you for living the rest of your life.

Liberal arts courses also give you an understanding of the shared values, customs, and institutions of our Western culture. The values they advocate are critical to the proper functioning of a democracy. With a liberal arts background, you will be better prepared to understand and intelligently debate the issues of the day, and you will more likely make wise decisions in all areas of your life.

The areas covered by the liberal arts curriculum have changed often since their initial formation in the time of the Greeks. However, their purpose in developing responsible citizens has never wavered. Presently the liberal arts curriculum covers four basic areas:

- Fine arts   Art, music, dance, theater

- Humanities   Literature, foreign languages, history, philosophy, religion

- Natural sciences   Mathematics, astronomy, geography, geology, physics, biology, chemistry

- Social sciences   Economics, sociology, psychology, political science, anthropology

The value of the liberal arts is expressed well in the 1996–1997 catalog of Lycoming College, a Pennsylvania liberal arts college founded in 1812:

> Lycoming College is committed to the principle that a liberal arts education is the ideal foundation for an informed and productive life. The liberal arts—including the fine arts, the humanities, mathematics, the natural and social sciences—have created the social, political, economic and intellectual systems which help define contemporary existence. Therefore it is essential that students grasp the modes of inquiry and knowledge associated with these disciplines. (p. 37)

THE VALUE OF THE LIBERAL ARTS TO YOUR EDUCATION

Many students look on their general education course requirements as unnecessary obstacles to obtaining their degree. Some liberal arts courses may force you to struggle with topics and methods of expression that are unfamiliar but ultimately will help you learn and grow. These courses reveal important areas of human knowledge that you might otherwise overlook. They can instill in you a love of learning and add pleasure to your life. Many scientists have developed a love of music or poetry while meeting their general education requirements for their college degrees. It is important to look at these courses as a way to broaden your understanding of life and the part you play in it.

▲ Understanding Your Reasons for Coming to College

You have seen why other people believe college is an important part of reaching their life goals. Now you have the opportunity to identify the reasons *you* believe college is important. To do this, complete the following exercises.

ACTIVE LEARNING

Exercise 2.1 *Split up into groups of three or four. As a group, review your school's general course catalog and answer the following questions:*

1. What is the mission statement of your school?

_____

_____

_____

_____

_____

2. What is the name of the set of core courses all students have to take to graduate? Briefly describe these graduation course requirements. List the courses your group would most likely take to meet this requirement and give reasons for selecting them. How closely do these course requirements resemble your college's liberal arts curriculum?

_____

_____

_____

_____

ACTIVE LEARNING

Exercise 2.2 *In the same groups as in Exercise 2.1, discuss the following issue: Is a liberal arts education really the ideal foundation for an informed and productive life? If your answer is* yes, *explain why. If your answer is* no, *give an alternative educational foundation.(Each group should be prepared to share its answers with the class. This would also make a good basis for a lively debate.)*

ACTIVE LEARNING

Exercise 2.3 *Write down at least three reasons why you are in college. Then answer the following questions:*

1. How committed are you to being successful in college? In life?

_____

_____

_____

_____

2. What role do you expect college to play in reaching your life goals? What role did your family and others play in your decision to attend college?

_____

_____

_____

_____

_____

Be prepared to share your answers with the class. (This exercise may also be used as a short speech of introduction.)

ACTIVE LEARNING

Exercise 2.4 *Interview a recent college graduate and ask how college changed him or her. What does this person think was the best part of college? The worst part? Does he or she believe college was worth the effort? Why or why not?*

ACTIVE LEARNING

Exercise 2.5 *Using the Internet, a newspaper, or some other source, find a want ad for three jobs that interest you. Write down what qualifications you would need to be hired for these jobs. Then describe what you are doing now to get those qualifications. Be prepared to share your findings with the class.*

_____

_____

_____

_____

_____

ETHICS

Exercise 2.6 *Pair off with a classmate. Share with your partner who most influences how you think. Describe the way that person influences the way you think at school, at home, and in public.*

ETHICS

Exercise 2.7 *In groups of four to six, make a list of various organizations, both in and out of government, that influence educational choices. Describe how these groups affect your personal educational choices.*

_____

_____

_____

_____

_____

DIVERSITY

Exercise 2.8 *In the same groups as in Exercise 2.7, make a list of at least three organizations that assist minority and physically challenged students. Discuss how these groups help these students complete their education. Discuss what changes you would make to these benefits to improve the overall student population at your school.*

_____

_____

_____

_____

_____

ACTIVE LEARNING

Exercise 2.9 *In groups of two or three, discuss the differences between education and training. When would training be the more effective way to improve your skills in your chosen field or major? When would education be the more valuable way?*

ACTIVE LEARNING

Exercise 2.10 *Write a short poem (at least eight lines) describing your reasons for coming to college.*

_____

_____

_____

_____

_____

_____

_____

WRITING

Exercise 2.11 *Write a letter to the editor of your college or local newspaper describing your college experience so far. (Be sure to follow the guidelines for letters to the editor found in the newspaper.)*

CHAPTER HIGHLIGHTS

1. Understanding why you are in college and what you want to gain from it can strengthen your personal commitment to finish your education. This is the first step in your overall success at school and in life.

2. For most people, reaching life goals means acquiring new skills and developing new talents beyond those provided by a high school education.

3. Your ability to compete in the job market will depend largely on whether you keep your skills and talents up to date.

4. Lifelong learning is something we all must do for the rest of our lives.

5. A foundation for a good post–high school education starts with learning the principles of critical thinking and problem solving. These principles are found in nearly all college courses.

6. The transitions from memorization to critical thinking and from passive to active learning are among the greatest benefits of college-level learning.

7. College offers the best place to "load up" on technical skills. It is also a good place to periodically "reload" your skills during your career.

8. An education can offer greater advantages than training.

9. Education should make you feel uncomfortable. Feeling uncomfortable means you are learning and growing.

10. For many people, the liberal arts provide the foundation for an informed and productive life.

CHAPTER HIGHLIGHTS

CASE STUDY
Juan's Great Confrontation

Juan could hear the music blasting halfway down the hall as he made his way back to his dorm room. This meant that Alberto, his roommate, was already finished studying for the day, and it was only 2:00 on Saturday afternoon. Juan had been gone since 9:00 that morning, meeting with his study group to finish writing their organic chemistry lab report that was due on Monday. Juan still had a lot of schoolwork to get done today.

In some ways, Juan envied his roommate's choice of a liberal arts major in American history. It seemed that every semester Alberto only had to write a couple of term papers for each class, attend a few lectures, and he was all set. Alberto was doing well in his classes because he wrote excellent papers. His professors just loved his writing. But someday Alberto would pay, Juan thought. Juan was convinced that his own hard work as a chemical engineering major would get him a top starting salary far above what Alberto would most likely receive.

After giving Alberto a hard time about his choice of music, Juan asked him for some advice about selecting a topic for a term paper in American literature. Alberto suggested a book called *Self-Reliance* by Ralph Waldo Emerson that he had read in a similar course last year. While Juan listened to Alberto talk about what the book had to say, he found himself intrigued by the topics of friendship, self-reliance, and character. He had always felt strongly about these issues, but had never read about them in a book.

Alberto kidded that Juan would be a lot better off taking more general education courses and fewer technical courses. "What I learn in these courses will last me a lifetime," he said, "while your technical education will be obsolete within five years after you earn your degree." However, Juan felt uncomfortable with liberal arts courses that were pulling down his grade-point average. These "mushy things" were okay to talk about in dorm discussions, but no one could really expect to make a living off of them. If the world was going to be better off, it would have to rely on things a lot more concrete than the stuff found in American literature courses. Technology, not liberal arts, would make the world a better place. That was why Juan had chosen a major in chemical engineering. The career prospects were also much better.

Although Juan thought he had won the argument about the value of technology over the liberal arts, several of Alberto's comments still troubled him. Would his first-rate technical knowledge really be completely obsolete five years after graduation? How could he prevent this from happening? Although he was reluctant to admit it to Alberto, Juan knew there was more to life than just technology, as he had learned from his days of playing the trumpet in his high school orchestra. But now, lab courses took so much of his time that he couldn't find time for anything else.

If you were Alberto, what would you tell Juan?

Personal Journal

SELF-AWARENESS

Personal Journal 2.1 Discuss how you think a college education will make a difference in your life. How will college affect your selection of life goals? How will it affect the quality of your life? Which aspect of the liberal arts most interests you? Why? What aspect of the liberal arts least interests you? Why?

_____

_____

_____

_____

_____

_____

_____

_____

DIVERSITY

Personal Journal 2.2 Write about why the liberal arts might be useful in a multicultural world. Do you think a liberal arts curriculum is broad enough to prepare you for the future? Why or why not? What would you change about the liberal arts curriculum, if anything? Should it be expanded or changed? How do you think the liberal arts will enrich your future? Be specific in your answers.

_____

_____

_____

_____

_____

_____

_____

CHAPTER QUIZ

1. Explain why education is a lifetime activity rather than something you do once and then get on with your life.

   _____

   _____

   _____

   _____

   _____

2. Discuss why the principles of critical thinking and problem solving are important to your success in life.

   _____

   _____

   _____

   _____

   _____

3. Describe how elementary and high school learning differ from college-level learning.

   _____

   _____

   _____

   _____

   _____

4. Discuss the role of the liberal arts in your education. Do you think a liberal arts degree alone is a worthwhile college goal? Explain your answer.

_____

_____

_____

_____

_____

5. Who had the greatest influence on how and what you thought in high school? Explain how this person had a positive or a negative effect on how you think today. If the person had a negative effect on your thinking, discuss what you are doing to change the way you think.

_____

_____

_____

_____

6. Is it possible for an outside group or organization to influence what you learn in college? Explain your answer and give examples.

_____

_____

_____

_____

ADDITIONAL RESOURCES

Covey, Stephen R. *Seven Habits of Very Effective People: Restoring the Character Ethic.* New York: Simon & Schuster, 1989.

Cronon, William. "Only Connect . . . ": The Goals of a Liberal Education," *The American Scholar*, Autumn 1998, pp. 73–80.

Dewey, John. *How We Think: A Restatement of the Relation of Reflective Thinking to the Educative Process*, 2d ed. Lexington, MA: D.C. Heath, 1960.

Emerson, Ralph Waldo. *Self-Reliance: The Wisdom of Ralph Waldo Emerson as Inspiration for Daily Living*, ed. Richard Whelan. New York: Crown Publishers, 1991.

CHAPTER 3

Time Management Skills

CHAPTER OBJECTIVES

After reading this chapter, you will understand why:

- Time is one of your most precious and most limited assets.
- Success in your life means managing your time.
- College and high school learning differ, which affects how you use your time in college.
- You need to make a daily time commitment to each college subject.

After reading this chapter, you will know how to:

- Develop weekly and semester time plans.
- Handle larger, long-term projects by:
    - Making Swiss cheese
    - Using time lines
    - Using to-do lists
    - Setting priorities
- Simplify your life.

Do you ever notice how successful people somehow accomplish a lot every day? Every person has the same amount of time available each day: 24 hours. Yet successful people get more done. How do they do it?

You may be wondering why you should even think about this during your college years. You may feel there aren't enough hours in the day for your demanding college schedule, but in reality you can accomplish a lot in 24 hours each day. You can join the successful people who make the most of their time.

College life affords you a great deal of freedom. If you choose to sleep until noon every day or to wear the same socks for the whole semester, you have the freedom to do it. In college, you have more freedom than ever before. At the same time, there are higher expectations for performance and greater demands on your time. Each course covers a large amount of material, and the pace of learning is much faster. Often you will cover more material in the first week of a college course than you did in a whole semester in high school.

The end of the semester seems far away, but by now several weeks have already passed. Time is racing along, and tests and projects are piling up. In the following weeks, your schedule will get very demanding. You may wonder how you will get it all done. You can easily become overwhelmed by such a workload, unless you have a plan—a plan that will help you successfully manage your time.

▲ Time Is Your Most Valuable Asset

You will quickly find that time is your most valuable asset. No matter how rich you become, you cannot buy more time, save time, or hoard it. When time has run out, it is gone. If you are not interested in managing your time, others will manage it for you. How you manage your time is an important part of becoming an effective and successful person.

▲ College Learning Versus High School Learning: Dealing with Ideas Versus Memorizing Facts

When you were in high school, being smart may have been all you needed to survive in school. College learning is different. Your professors probably will not ask you to memorize 10 spelling words or 15 kinds of spiders for a quiz.

More than likely, they will ask you to synthesize and analyze ideas, and be able to explain them concisely and coherently in essay exams and research papers. They will assign you papers and projects at the beginning of the semester and not mention them again until they are due. Your grade for the whole semester may rest on your performance on a single examination or research paper.

To do well in a college course requires a daily time commitment for the entire term. College-level learning requires you to reprocess information, which you cannot do by cramming the night before a test. Even if you do cram facts into your mind, they rarely stay there. As a general rule, two hours of study time outside of class for each hour of class time is sufficient. For instance, if you carry 15 credits in a semester, you will need to study 30 hours each week. Class time and study time give you a total of 45 hours per week that you devote to school. You may ask: How can I do this and still have a life? But this schedule is very feasible once you learn to manage your time. With a little planning and discipline on your part, the payoff will be enormous.

Exercise 3.1A *This exercise is a timed test of your ability to process information. Place your pencil at the number 1 in the upper left part of Figure 3.1A. When told to begin, draw a line from number 1 to number 2, from number 2 to number 3, and so on until you reach number 60 or until time runs out. You have 60 seconds to complete this exercise. Circle the highest number you reach.*

17   40   28
1   49   6
13   37   16   26
25   54
3   50
29   30
51
5   39   42 14   2
27   15   18
52
53   41   38   4
21   48
59
19   58
47   45   36   34
31
10
7   57   60
43   20
35   56
8
23   44
32
11   55   22
24
33
9   12   46

FIGURE 3.1A 1–60 Number System

ACTIVE LEARNING

Exercise 3.1B *You will take the same timed test that you took in Exercise 3.1A, but this time you have the following new information. The odd numbers (1, 3, 5, . . .) are always on the left, and the even numbers (2, 4, 6, . . .) are always on the right. The numbers are in groups of six that alternate between the top and bottom of the figure. (For example, numbers 1 through 6 are found on the top half of the figure, numbers 7 through 12 on the bottom half, numbers 13 through 18 on the top half, and so on.) Now, armed with this new information, take this one-minute test again in Figure 3.1B on page 44. Circle the highest number you reach.*

What is the difference in the results of the two tests? Did you do better the second time? Most likely you did, because this time you had a plan that helped you attack the problem. Instead of searching frantically for the next number as you did on the first test, you narrowed your search on the second test by using the information given. Having a plan makes you more efficient and saves you time.

17
    1   49   40   6   28
13   37   16 26
   25   54
3   50
   29   30
51
5   39   42 14   2
27   15   18
            52
53   41   38   4
  21   48
      59
19   58
 47   45   36   34
   31
             10
 7   57   60
      43   20
  35   56
        8
23   44
        32
  11   55   22
          24
   33
9   12 46

FIGURE 3.1B 1–60 Number System Revisited

▲ *Developing a Time Plan*

Exercise 3.2 *Begin your time planning by writing down everything you do during the next week. Using the chart in Figure 3.2, summarize how you spend each day of your week. It does not have to be perfect.*

FIGURE 3.2 One-Week Time Record

Category	Monday	Tuesday	Wednesday	Thursday	Friday	Saturday	Sunday	Total
Sleeping								
Eating								
Relaxing								
Working								
Exercising								
Commuting								
Studying								
Family time								
Class time								
Self time								
Total	24 hours	24 hours	24 hours	24 hours	24 hours	24 hours	24 hours	168 hours

ACTIVE LEARNING

Exercise 3.3 *Once you have completed your one-week time record in Figure 3.2, analyze the results. Using the time use analysis sheet in Figure 3.3, mark the areas where you think you are spending too little time and too much time. Explain how you feel about your overall use of time. (For instance, did you honestly spend two hours of study time for each hour of class time in each course? Your answers may surprise you.) List the changes you would like to make and how you will carry them out. Remember, there are no right or wrong answers; the answers matter only to you.*

To see what a successful weekly schedule looks like, look at Tiffany's weekly planner (see Figure 3.4) to see how she used her time. Tiffany has a 16-credit course load with one laboratory course and works 10 hours a week. Her weekly planning begins by entering the nonnegotiable items, such as classes and work. She schedules a 20-minute preparation period *before each class* and a 20-minute review period *after each class* so she can move data from her short-term memory to her long-term memory with short study periods.

FIGURE 3.3 Time Use Analysis

1. Mark the areas where you feel you are spending *too little time*

   ❏ Sleeping   ❏ Relaxing   ❏ Exercising   ❏ Studying

   ❏ Class time   ❏ Eating   ❏ Working   ❏ Commuting

   ❏ Family time   ❏ Self time

2. Mark the areas where you feel you are spending *too much time*

   ❏ Sleeping   ❏ Relaxing   ❏ Exercising   ❏ Studying

   ❏ Class time   ❏ Eating   ❏ Working   ❏ Commuting

   ❏ Family time   ❏ Self time

3. How do you feel about your overall use of time?

4. What changes do you want to make in your time use?

5. How do you plan to change your use of time?

6. How many hours of study time do you spend for each hour you are in class? How will you manage your time to bring it up to what it should be (about 2 hours of study time for each hour in class)?

Tiffany studies before class to make sure the material for that day is fresh in her mind when the class begins. She finds it easier to pinpoint areas of confusion so she can pay closer attention to them in class and ask the professor about them. Her after-class review period is designed to reinforce what she learned that day. She also finds it is a great time to clean up her notes and to clarify her understanding. If something does not make sense, she talks it over with a classmate or contacts her professor during office hours. The sooner she gets the information set correctly in her mind, the more likely she will remember it correctly at test time.

FIGURE 3.4 **Tiffany's Weekly Planner**

Time	Monday	Tuesday	Wednesday	Thursday	Friday	Saturday	Sunday
7 A.M.	Get Up P-Bio	Get Up	Get Up	Get Up	Get Up P-Bio	Get Up	Open
8 A.M.	Bio Lect	Breakfast	Breakfast	Breakfast	Bio Lect	Breakfast	Open
9 A.M.	Breakfast	Open P-French	Study	Open P-French	Breakfast	Study	Open
10 A.M.	R-Bio P-English	French	Study P-English	French	R-Bio P-English	Study	Open
11 A.M.	English	French R-French	English	French R-French	English	Study	Open
Noon	R-English Lunch	Lunch	R-English Lunch	Lunch	R-English Lunch	Lunch	Open
1 P.M.	P-Econ P-History	Open	P-Econ P-History	Work	P-Econ P-History	Work	Open
2 P.M.	Econ	Open P-Bio	Econ	Work	Econ	Work	Open
3 P.M.	History	Bio Lab	History	Work	History	Work	Open
4 P.M.	R-Econ R-History	Bio Lab	R-Econ R-History	Work	R-Econ R-History	Work	Open
5 P.M.	Exercise	Bio Lab R-Bio Lab	Exercise	Work	Exercise	Work	Open
6 P.M.	Dinner	Dinner	Dinner	Dinner	Dinner	Dinner	Dinner
7 P.M.	Study	Study	Study	Study	Study	Social	Study
8 P.M.	Study	Study	Study	Study	Study	Social	Study
9 P.M.	Study	Study	Study	Study	Study	Social	Study
10 P.M.	Open	Open	Open	Open	Open	Social	Open
11 P.M.	Bed	Bed	Bed	Bed	Bed	Social	Bed
Midnight						Bed	

P = Preparation Time   R = Review Time

Next, Tiffany fills in her study time. She counts the 20 minutes before and after class as part of her two hours of study time per hour of class time for each course. Because of flexible college schedules, she can program her study time during daylight hours and take advantage of breaks between classes to lighten her evening study load. In the example, Tiffany has reduced her nighttime study load from about five hours to three hours by studying two hours during the day. This allows her to finish studying by 10:00 P.M. so she can get the sleep she needs to be alert in class and avoid getting run down.

It is important for you to schedule class time, study time, and work time first, since they are the highest-priority items. Once they are set, you can fill in meal times, exercise times, social time, and so on. In Tiffany's case, she fits everything into her week and still has Saturday night and most of Sunday free. Because she has to work, she decides to study Friday night so she can relax and socialize most of Sunday. If she wanted Friday night to socialize, she could trade it off for study time on Sunday. The choice is hers. She realizes, however, that her time is limited, and she must make choices to achieve her life goal of earning a college degree.

Exercise 3.4 *Now it is time for you to make your own weekly schedule. Using the chart in Figure 3.5, make a plan for next week. Remember to fill in the top-priority items first. Don't forget other items like meals, personal hygiene, and social time. Then put your planner in a place where you can see it every day. Carry a copy with you to remind you of what you are supposed to be doing. Also, make a copy of the blank planner in Figure 3.5 so you can keep track of how you actually spend your time during the coming week. At the end of the week, compare the two planners.*

When you analyze the differences between your two planners—how you planned to spend your time and how you actually spent it—do not be too harsh on yourself. Try to come closer to your plan each week, and soon you will greatly improve your use of time. Along the way, you will learn a lot about yourself and what keeps you from sticking to your time goals. For example, are you spending too much time on some things and not enough on others? In some

FIGURE 3.5 My Weekly Planner

Time	Monday	Tuesday	Wednesday	Thursday	Friday	Saturday	Sunday
6 A.M.							
7 A.M.							
8 A.M.							
9 A.M.							
10 A.M.							
11 A.M.							
Noon							
1 P.M.							
2 P.M.							
3 P.M.							
4 P.M.							
5 P.M.							
6 P.M.							
7 P.M.							
8 P.M.							
9 P.M.							
10 P.M.							
11 P.M.							
Midnight							

courses, you may find that the two-to-one ratio between study time and class time is too large, or perhaps it is not large enough. Then you can adjust your planner. Analyze your time use at the end of each week. By the end of the semester, you will be in control of your time, and you will be reaching your goals.

Next, you need to discover what the "time bandits" are doing to your plan. Time bandits are distractions that steal away your time and prevent you from carrying out your time management plan (see Figure 3.6). What are your time bandits? Are they noisy roommates? Friends interrupting your study time? Finding a quiet place to study? General procrastination? An unpredictable work schedule?

Once you have identified your time bandits, you can find ways to eliminate them. A good first step is to establish an official study area. If your dorm room or apartment is not a good place to study, search for a better place. You might find a special place in the library (such as an area back in the stacks) or in an empty classroom.

Make sure to stock your official study area with pens, pencils, staplers, rulers, and so forth, and get a special study bag or backpack to transport them if necessary. Ideally, try to use the same spot each time so the chair, lighting, and table or desk are optimal for you. When you arrive at your official study area, it should say to you, "Let's get to work!"

SEMESTER PLANNING

Another critical part of time management is looking at the big picture—the whole semester. You can get a calendar that has the entire month on a single page. Some larger wall calendars may display your entire semester at a glance. Look at the month-at-a-glance planner in Figure 3.7. When the semester begins, write in the due dates for all your projects and reports and the dates for all exams for each month. Hang a copy of your planner in your official study area so you can see it every day, and carry another copy with you. This will help you visualize the big events of the semester and prevent them from sneaking up on you.

FIGURE 3.6 The Time Bandits

- Noisy roommates
- Telephone calls
- Traffic noise
- Surprise visitors
- The Internet
- Video games
- email
- Television
- Computer games
- Sports

FIGURE 3.7 **Month-at-a-Glance Planner**

MONTH

Sunday	Monday	Tuesday	Wednesday	Thursday	Friday	Saturday

ACTIVE LEARNING

Exercise 3.5 *Develop your own semester-at-a-glance planner for this semester. Use as many monthly calendars as you need to enter all the dates for your papers, exams, projects, lab reports, and any other major due dates. Write down other big events such as birthdays, social events, and things you do not want to miss. Be sure your weekly planners do not conflict with your semester planner.*

SCHEDULING GUIDELINES

The purpose of managing your time is to give order to your life, help you accomplish your goals, and bring satisfaction to your life. Time management not only helps you accomplish the things that matter most to you but also helps you realize that time is not endless. Like anything else in life that has value, time requires your attention and management. Through sound planning, you can do more of the things that are really important to you. Reward yourself when you succeed. If you get an *A* on the economics test, skip the next study period for economics and go to a movie—you earned it! Be sure to schedule social time, personal ("me") time, and recreational time. These are all important parts of your long-run success.

It is important to remember that setbacks will occur. Be reasonable with yourself. You may get sick, or things beyond your control may disrupt your time plan. Remember to be flexible and bounce back from these occurrences. Above all, be strong when people and circumstances interrupt your plan. When friends call during your study time, tell them you will call them back later. If you have trouble eliminating distractions during a study time, move to another study area. Time management helps you overcome the obstacles to success rather than avoid them. Time bandits will always be there, but you can move them aside and get on with your success.

▲ *How to Handle Long-Term and Big Projects*

KNOWING WHAT NEEDS TO BE DONE

The first step in any project is to know what you have to do. If there are instructions, you need to read them carefully and then read them again. The same applies to class assignments. If you write down assignments in your own words, you will increase your understanding of each assignment and take personal ownership of what has to be done. If possible, verify your understanding of the assignment by explaining it back to your professor in your own words. This is a great way to clarify what the professor expects, clear up misconceptions, and avoid wasting time on unnecessary work. You will maximize the results from your time and effort.

ACTIVE LEARNING

Exercise 3.6 *Take the timed test of ability to follow written instructions in Figure 3.8. You have just three minutes to complete the test. You must follow all written instructions completely to receive full credit.*

This exercise may seem trivial, but it makes a big point. Reading directions and thinking before you jump into a project can save you a lot of time and effort. Thinking before you act and planning before you do something are two ways to be more efficient.

FIGURE 3.8 **Timed Aptitude Test**

Name:_____

Note: This is a timed test. You will be permitted just *three (3) minutes* to receive full credit if you complete each item.

Can You Follow Directions?

1. Read everything carefully before doing anything.

2. Write your last name in the upper left-hand corner of this sheet.

3. Draw a circle around the word *name* in the second sentence.

4. Draw five small squares in the upper right-hand corner of this sheet.

5. Place an *X* in each square made in number 4.

6. Call out your first name when you read this sentence.

7. Print *yes* after the title at the top of this sheet.

8. Mark an *X* in the lower left-hand corner of this sheet.

9. Draw a circle completely around the sentence in number 7.

10. Multiply 70 by 61 on the back of this sheet.

11. Call out "I have" if you think you have followed all directions to this point.

12. Circle all even numbers on the sheet.

13. Write the numbers 1 to 10 in reverse order on the bottom of this page.

14. Draw a square around each number that is written on this page.

15. Follow just the directions given in items 1 and 2.

DIVERSITY

Exercise 3.7 *People with physical or learning disabilities may need extra time or assistance during a test. Pair up with another student in your class. Keeping your eyes closed the entire time, make your weekly planner for next week. Be sure to prioritize your tasks and include class times, study times, and other activities. You can ask your partner to write for you or look up things in your notebook, but you must come up with all the information for the planner. Compare this experience with your experience in Exercise 3.4, where you filled out your planner with your eyes open. How much more time did it take this time? How did you feel about communicating your ideas to someone else and trusting him or her to fill out your* *planner? How will you use the planner your partner wrote out for you if you can not see it? Does this experience change the way you perceive students who have disabilities? Explain.*

MAKING SWISS CHEESE OUT OF PROJECTS

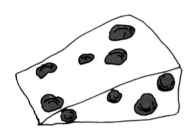

Alan Lakein, noted time management expert, recommends making "Swiss cheese" out of your project.[1] Swiss cheese is unique because it is full of holes. As a result, there is less cheese than appears from the outside; the holes actually reduce the size of the portion of cheese. The same is true of a large or long-term project. If you feel instantly overwhelmed by a big project, just carve a few holes out of it—that is, reduce the overall project to a series of smaller, more manageable projects.

The third step in project development is to establish a time line for your project. Once you have broken down your project into a series of smaller tasks, you can arrange these tasks into a logical sequence and assign them start and finish dates. Figure 3.9 illustrates how to set up a time line for a research paper. Notice that the time line has several time breaks and a completion date the week before the due date. This schedule allows for unanticipated interruptions such as getting the flu the week before your paper is due.

USING TO-DO LISTS

Although you cannot "do" a goal, you can list the things you need to do to accomplish it. These are often small, individual tasks, but collectively they will accomplish your goal. They can be simple things like making a telephone call to order an important book so it will arrive in plenty of time, or sending an email to a trusted source. The idea is to move closer to your goal each day of the semester.

You probably followed this method for completing a long-term project when you successfully got into the college of your choice. You started your to-do list to get into college many years ago (see Figure 3.10). The first thing you

---

1. Alan Lakein, *How to Get Control of Your Time and Your Life* (New York: Signet Books, 1996).

FIGURE 3.9 Project Time Line

Week 1	Receive semester project description from professor
	Listen to class discussion of what is expected
	Ask professor questions to clarify what is expected
Weeks 2–4	Begin search for topic
	Develop topic for paper
	Develop tentative outline for paper
Week 5	Submit tentative topic and outline to professor
Week 6	Meet with professor to discuss topic and paper outline
Week 7	Submit revised outline to professor
Week 8	Meet with professor to get final approval of topic and paper outline
Weeks 9–11	Develop first draft of paper
Week 12	Develop second draft of paper
Week 13	Develop third draft of paper
Week 14	Prepare final paper
Week 15	Turn in finished paper

did was enroll in college preparatory courses in high school. Next, you worked to get good grades in high school. Next, you took the SAT or the ACT. Before long, you decided what schools you wanted to apply to, requested applications from those schools, filled out the applications, and got letters of recommendation. Finally, you mailed the completed applications to the colleges.

These steps would make a good to-do list or a time line. You successfully broke down your long-term goal into smaller, more manageable parts. You made Swiss cheese out of it.

SETTING PRIORITIES

Everything on your to-do list was an important step in accomplishing your long-term goal of getting into college. Goals are valuable because they force you to focus your attention. In this case, the process was simple since you were concentrating on a single goal. Fortunately, life is not that dull and not nearly that simple. Normally you want to accomplish a host of things in your life. You want close friends, good health, a happy family, a rewarding career, and financial success. These goals require a major commitment of your time, money, and energy.

FIGURE 3.10 **My To-Do List to Get into College**

Long-Term Life Goal: Get a College Degree

  Intermediate Goal 1: Get into College

    My To-Do List to Get into College

    1. Take college preparatory courses

    2. Get good grades in high school classes

    3. Take SAT or ACT

    4. Select colleges I wish to attend

    5. Visit colleges

    6. Send for college applications

    7. Fill out college applications and get letters of recommendation

    8. Send applications to colleges

  My Time Line

To-Do List Item	When It Needs to Be Done
1. Take college preparatory courses	Sign up in grade 8
2. Get good grades in high school	Grades 9 to 12
3. Take SAT or ACT	Spring of grade 11, fall of grade 12
4. Select colleges I wish to attend	Spring of grade 11
5. Visit colleges	Summer before grade 12
6. Send for college applications	September of grade 12
7. Fill out applications; get letters of recommendation	October of grade 12
8. Send applications to colleges	November of grade 12

Most likely you will not have enough time, money, or energy to achieve all these goals simultaneously, but they are probably all possible with some sound planning and the right set of priorities.

Time management expert Alan Lakein recommends that people establish life priorities. Simply put, you need to decide what is important to you and what is not. To some people, everything seems important; to others, nothing seems important. As with most things in life, the best answer rests in the middle. The secret to success is very simple: devote your time, money, and energy to the things that are most important to you. Try assessing what is important to other people by observing how they spend their time, money, and energy. Look back at how you spent your time in Exercises 3.2, 3.3, and 3.4. What seems to be your priorities? What do you value most? If what you learned about yourself surprises you or concerns you, now is a great time to change how you spend your time. You might want to show a classmate your weekly or semester planner and ask this person what she or he thinks is important to you by looking at your calendar.

BE AN *A* STUDENT

Now it is time to translate your long-term goals into semester, weekly, and daily time-use plans. Make a *semester time plan* by using your semester-at-a-glance planner from Exercise 3.5, which should be hanging in your official study area. Make your *weekly time plan* from Exercise 3.4, which should also be hanging in that area. Then you will be able to make a *daily time plan* that will help you decide what to do in the time blocks that you have devoted to studying. You can call this your *daily to-do list.*

Alan Lakein recommends that at the end of each day you make a to-do list that includes the things you need to do the next day to accomplish your goals. Prioritize these tasks by putting an *A* next to the items that are most important to your life goals. Put a *B* next to those that are moderately important, and put a *C* next to those that are least important.

The next step is to move the things in the *B* category into either the *A* or *C* category. What you spend your time doing is either important or not. Don't allow yourself to have tasks that are neutral in the *B* category.

Now put the list of *C* items out of your sight, such as in a desk drawer. (But remember where you put it in case you ever need them.) Next, spend your time working on the *A* items. These are the things that will help you accomplish your long-term life goals. The world is full of people who spend most of their lives working on *C* items. These people work very hard, but are frustrated because they never realize their life goals. Remember to be an *A* student who works mainly on *A* items.

If this system seems overwhelming, keep in mind that you will be making up a new to-do list each day. Today's *C* item can become an *A* item tomorrow. For example, calling your mother might be a *C* item today, but if your roommate tells you that your mother called with some important news, it suddenly becomes an *A* item. Usually, however, your *C* items don't change very much.

This priority system keeps you focused and working on the most important items rather than spending your time on tasks that can wait. Lakein suggests that you always ask yourself this question: What is the best use of my time right now? Sometimes your schedule says to study, but your body says to sleep. If you really need to sleep, your proper response is to sleep and make up the study time later. Be flexible. Be realistic. Be an *A* student!

▲ *Simplify Your Life*

Keeping your life simple is another way to stay focused on the important tasks needed to accomplish your long-run goals. Here are some ways to simplify your life:

- *Learn to say* **no** *to unnecessary commitments.* A good way to test yourself is to ask: Do I feel more guilty saying *yes* or saying *no*? If saying *yes* makes you feel more guilty, you probably should say *no*.

- *When you run errands, do several in one trip.* Making a to-do list for your errands may help. Be sure to keep it posted where you can find it when you go.

- *At the start of the semester, mark all birthdays, anniversaries, and other important dates on your semester-at-a-glance calendar.* (See Exercise 3.5.)

- *At the start of the semester, buy a bunch of birthday cards and other greeting cards.* Do not forget the stamps. When you remember a birthday or another occasion, you will have everything you need to respond quickly.

- *Make appointments whenever you can.* For recurring appointments such as haircuts, make the appointment for the next one while you are getting one done. This spares you from sitting around waiting for your turn.

- *Carry some of your schoolwork with you.* Then you can study whenever you have a spare moment, such as while waiting for an appointment.

- *Keep a three-ring binder for each course.* Organize all the papers and handouts for that course in the binder so you can find something when you need it.

- *Learn to rough-sort your books and backup material.* For example, put all your English course backup materials (library books, research materials for papers) in the first drawer of your desk, your psychology course materials in the second drawer, and so on. This kind of sorting system requires little effort and greatly reduces the number of places you have to look for something.

- *Put things back where they belong.* You can stay organized only by heeding that age-old advice to put things back in their proper places.

You are quickly learning that time is your most valuable asset. In this chapter, you have seen how your life runs more smoothly and is more satisfying if you manage your time well. You have also learned why time management is more important to you now than ever before. Good time management and well-organized priorities are often the difference between a good student and a poor student. By utilizing the time and project management techniques presented in this chapter, you will soon be making the most of the time in your life.

CHAPTER HIGHLIGHTS

1. Whereas high school learning relies heavily on memorization, college learning requires you to synthesize ideas and explain them coherently to others, either orally or in writing.

2. To synthesize ideas successfully, you must make a daily time commitment in each course for the entire semester rather than cramming everything in at the last moment.

3. Time is one of your most precious and limited assets.

4. Success in life starts by managing your time.

5. Good time management begins with developing a semester, weekly, and daily time plan that you commit to follow.

6. Long-term and large projects require special handling and planning. Three good techniques are making Swiss cheese, creating time lines, and using to-do lists.

7. Always strive to be an *A* student by setting priorities and working only on *A* items. *A* items are top-priority things that help you accomplish your life goals.

8. Keep your life simple so you can have more time to work on your *A* items.

CHAPTER HIGHLIGHTS

CASE STUDY
Kendra's Big Time Dilemma

It was just after 4:00 P.M. on a beautiful Friday afternoon as Kendra was walking back from her last class. A college freshman, she had just completed her first full week of classes and was looking forward to catching up on her sleep and doing a little partying over the weekend.

Kendra had been up until at least 2:00 A.M. every night this week, and she was already behind in several courses. She wondered if she could not keep up during the first week, how would she make it through the semester? Being able to sleep the weekend away offered her a chance to conserve her energy so she could catch up on her work next week. Kendra did not have to be at her library job until 1:00 P.M. on Saturday. She felt fortunate to have found a job there for 10 hours a week during the school year. The money she earned paid for her laundry and other incidental weekly expenses.

As she walked along, she started thinking about her first week of classes. Some of her courses seemed like they might be fun. She also thought about all the things her professors had assigned already this semester. It seemed as though each professor thought his or her course was the only one she was taking. Didn't they realize she was carrying 16 credits this semester, including a biology lab every Tuesday afternoon? Kendra's history professor assigned at least 300 pages of reading each week. She had to write a research paper that counted as one-third of her grade, but fortunately it was not due until the last week of the semester. The economics course did not require much reading, but it sure took a lot of time to figure out what was going on. Luckily, Kendra had good English teachers in high school who stressed writing skills, so she would have little trouble writing the five-page paper that was due each Friday in freshman composition. Because she had done well on the foreign language placement test, Kendra skipped French I and enrolled in French II. One semester of a language and she would be finished with that graduation requirement. The only problem with the course was that she had to learn a huge number of vocabulary terms during the semester, and the professor gave periodic quizzes to measure students' mastery of all the new words.

As she reflected on all this work, Kendra felt overwhelmed and frustrated. It seemed as though she would have no time for anything but school and work. Wasn't college supposed to be fun? She remembered how refreshed she felt after her high school aerobics classes. How would she find time for exercise when there was not enough time to get her schoolwork done? She brought her workout clothes with her to school, but they were still in a gym bag in the back of her closet.

In high school, Kendra never studied more than 90 minutes a night, and she did very well. She even had time for lots of other things. College was not turning out at all like she thought it would. When Kendra got to her dorm, she sat on the bench outside to soak up some sun and think about how she could overcome her big-time dilemma.

If Kendra asked you for some advice on how to overcome her time dilemma, what would you tell her?

Personal Journal

SELF-AWARENESS

Personal Journal 3.1 Describe an experience in your life when you succeeded because of good planning. How did you feel about this accomplishment?

_____

_____

_____

_____

_____

_____

_____

_____

_____

SELF-AWARENESS

Personal Journal 3.2 Describe an experience in your life when you tried to accomplish something and failed because you did not think it through before-hand. How did you feel about this? What would you do differently if you had the chance to try it again? What did you learn from your success and from your failure that will help you in college and later in life?

_____

_____

_____

_____

_____

_____

_____

_____

_____

DIVERSITY

Personal Journal 3.3 Americans seem to worry a lot about time. How do you think Americans try to manage their time? What kind of time management is better: *efficient* time management (getting the most out of time spent) or *effective* time management (working on the most important things first)? How do you think people in other parts of the world view time management? Reflect on your own travels abroad, or talk to people from other countries about how citizens in those countries manage their time. Based on what you learned, do you think Americans manage their time well? Explain your answer.

_____

_____

_____

_____

_____

_____

_____

_____

CHAPTER QUIZ

1. Explain the difference between studying to memorize facts and studying to synthesize and analyze ideas.

   _____

   _____

   _____

   _____

   _____

2. What are some advantages of studying a subject each day as well as before and after each class?

   _____

   _____

   _____

   _____

   _____

3. Why are time lines and to-do lists important for a successful semester study plan?

   _____

   _____

   _____

   _____

   _____

4. Why is it better to work only on *A* items and put *C* items out of sight? Explain what happens to your *B* items when you prioritize.

_____

_____

_____

_____

_____

ADDITIONAL RESOURCES

Covey, Stephen R., A. Roger Merrill, and Rebecca R. Merrill. *First Things First.* New York: Simon & Schuster, 1995.

Lakein, Alan. *How to Get Control of Your Time and Your Life.* New York: Signet Books, 1996.

CHAPTER 4

Note-Taking Skills

After reading this chapter, you will understand why:

- Good note taking is important to college success.
- Good note taking is an extension of the principles of active learning.

After reading this chapter, you will know how to:

- Prepare before class to take good notes.
- Take good notes during class.
- Transform your class notes into a useful study guide after class.
- Use the Cornell note-taking style.
- Apply classroom note-taking techniques to outside readings.

Most college students claim that one of their least favorite activities is sitting through a boring lecture and taking notes. However, successful note taking is an important part of your classroom success, since most college examinations are based on what is presented in class. By developing good note-taking skills, you will get the most out of your classes and be able to prepare effectively for tests.

Taking good notes is easy when a professor gives clear reading assignments that provide a valuable background to an entertaining, well-organized lecture. On the other hand, taking notes can be very difficult when the reading assignments have nothing to do with what the professor covers in class, or when the lectures are disorganized and bear little resemblance to what the professor includes on the tests. No matter how the information is presented in class, however, you are still responsible for getting it right.

One problem with good note taking is that a well-done classroom lecture can be very deceiving and leave you with a false sense of security. For instance, everything a professor says and puts on the board may flow logically and make perfect sense. While your professor does all the work, you just write it down, usually without thinking about it. After all, you assume you will be able to think about it later. To reduce the chances of missing anything important, you write down each and every point, figuring that you will sort out what is important later. Since you are writing down everything, you devote your full attention to writing quickly. Even if you cannot read everything right now, you know it is okay since you can fix it later.

Unfortunately, when *later* arrives, you find yourself confused and frustrated with your notes and unsure about what you learned. You cannot read a lot of your own handwriting, and the sentences and phrases do not make much sense. How did you get yourself in this mess? There must be a better way to take notes.

Good note taking is actually an extension of the principles of critical thinking and active learning. Good note taking also requires a personal commitment to success. If you are willing to make that commitment, this chapter will help you get the most out of each class as well as prepare for tests.

This chapter is divided into three parts: what to do before, during, and after class. By following the simple principles and suggestions in this chapter, you will increase the quality of your class notes, decrease the quantity of your notes, and enhance the effectiveness of your test preparation.

▲ *What to Do Before Class*

Good preparation is the main source of success for most of the things you do in life. Good preparation is also necessary for effective note-taking skills. First, you need a basic understanding of how learning takes place. Knowledge is not directly transferred from your professor's mind to yours. When a direct transfer occurs, it normally involves only memorization, not knowledge. You memorize when your professor gives a list of the 50 state capitals and says there will be a quiz next week demanding you to write them down from memory. But you reach a higher level of critical thinking when you can write an essay in which you identify and describe the common forces surrounding the selection of the cities that became state capitals. It is not the professor's job to educate you; you must do that for yourself. You must be an active participant in your own learning.

A transfer of knowledge involves more than the transmission of information. For a knowledge transfer to occur, a teacher must disassemble his or her mind map of the subject (how things are organized in the mind) and logically impart it to students one piece at a time. If this transfer is successful, students will perceive the information clearly and begin to build their own mind maps of the material. Knowledge transfer goes much further than memorization because the information must pass through the brain of both teacher and student, who are both actively learning. This means the teacher must come to class ready to teach, and students must come ready to learn.

If you are an active learner, you do the following before going to class:

Complete all outside assignments before class. Before coming to class, look over the reading assignments and try to do the problems that will be covered. Remember that professors use outside assignments to introduce you to new material so you can spend class time refining the material, deciding what is important, and integrating new information. Before each class, you should already have started your own mind map of the material. You know where the gaps are in your understanding, and you actively listen for the missing pieces of information. When you arrive in class as an active learner, you are not seeing the material for the first time. You already have a good grasp of the major ideas.

Review your notes from the previous class and your outside assignments just before class. A last-minute review before class helps you to focus your thoughts on the material at hand. The review session does not have to be extensive; five to ten minutes is enough. You can make this process even more effective by using the Cornell note-taking style explained later in the chapter. You may be surprised to learn that most professors take 20 to 30 minutes before teaching a class to review their presentations and focus their minds on what they will teach. If you have several classes in a row, try to get to each class as quickly as possible and use the extra time to review.

Find a seat near the front center of the room. If you carefully choose your seat, you will reduce the number of distractions around you. Sitting in the front center lets you see well and hear clearly what is going on.

Bring the proper materials to class each day. This seems obvious, but you will hinder your commitment to learn if you do not have what you need in class every day.

▲ What to Do During Class

If you are completely prepared before class, you are ready to learn during class. You know what you are going to do in today's class *before* it starts. You have completed your outside assignments, and you may be coming to class with questions about the material. This attitude takes you out of the category of a passive recorder of information and into the category of an active learner. If you are an active learner, you do the following things during class:

Constantly evaluate the material being presented. You actively look for the big picture, the things that support it, and how the data connect to each other. Since you have already started your own mind map of the material before class and know where the gaps in your understanding are, you will easily find what you are looking for during class. The process works best when professors give well-planned lectures, but you can also find what you are seeking in a disorganized lecture.

Use the Cornell note-taking style. The Cornell note-taking style is an easy and effective way to incorporate active learning into your note taking. The Cornell format suggests that you set up your paper with a wide left-hand margin of 1 to 2½ inches. The section in the left margin (divided by a hand-drawn vertical line) is left blank for now. After class, you fill in this area with key words and phrases that will later trigger your memory about what you wrote on the right side of the line. To the right of the line is where you take your class notes.

Write down all specific items (definitions, formulas, dates). Although you usually would not write down every word the professor says, there are times when you should. You should write down every word of a definition or a formula, and all diagrams, dates, names, and numbers should be exact. You will know these are important because your professor will probably put them on the board. This type of information typically ends up as material for true-false, fill-in-the-blank, and multiple-choice questions. They can also help to ensure you get full credit when they are used as part of an essay question.

Leave lots of white space in your notes. As you take notes, spread things out. Do not be afraid to leave lots of space between items on the page. Later you can fill in these spaces with new information or insights about what you learned in class without disrupting the flow of your notes.

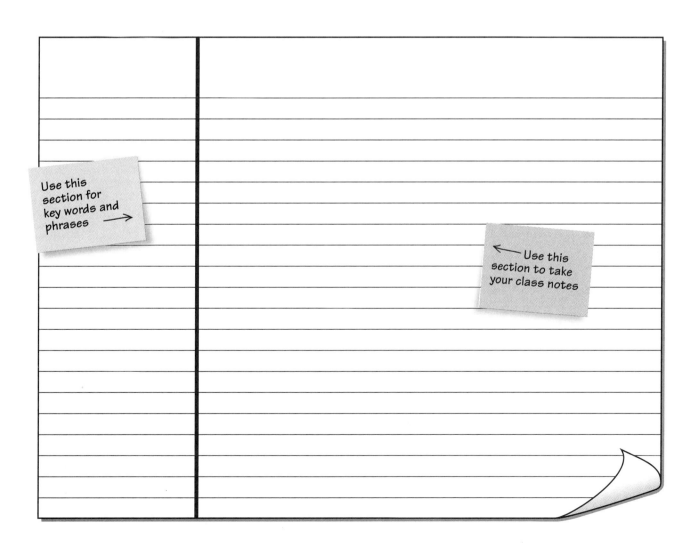

Mark each page of your notes with the date, page number, subject, and course name. If you happen to drop your notes or put them in the wrong place, you can quickly reassemble them in proper order and be sure you have everything.

Use a three-ring binder for each course. For each course, use a three-ring binder for your class notes, course syllabus, handouts, exams, quizzes, and anything else from the course. Use dividers to separate the various parts of the notebook (one part for notes, one for handouts, and so on). Set it up any way that makes sense to you. Some students carry a small paper punch so they can quickly and permanently put new materials in their notebooks during class. This reduces the chance of losing things.

Write on one side of the paper. This makes your notes easier to read and gives you greater flexibility in organizing and using your notes.

Use pictures, diagrams, and other artwork. Graphics help you visualize what you are learning and will increase your ability to remember data and concepts. A diagram that you draw of what you are learning is often called a *mind map*.

Use abbreviations, shorthand, and symbols. Most people have their own forms of shorthand to take notes more quickly. Be sure to write down all your symbols so you can remember what they mean. Some standard ones include:

=>   implies or causes

>   greater than

<   less than

b/c   because

Feel free to add your own symbols to this list.

Listen for clues from your professors. Most professors give strong hints about what they feel is important in a course. A few are more subtle, and you must listen very carefully. Others are very direct and say things such as "This will be on the test." Listen for what your professor repeats several times, and mark your notes accordingly.

▲ What to Do After Class

Applying your active learning continues even after class is over. What you do with the class material will determine your level of comprehension and your early preparation for the next test. If you are truly committed to success, you will do the following things after class:

Review your notes within 24 hours of class. If you wait more than 24 hours to review your notes, you will likely forget as much as 70 percent of what you learned. The review process begins right after class when you clean up your notes. Make sure you can read each word clearly and that you understand all your abbreviations. Translate words and phrases into meaningful sentences. Some students recopy their notes not only to help make them easier to read but also to be better able to recall the material later.

Use color-coded highlighting or some other system to identify different categories of material. Using colored highlighters will help you organize your notes to find things quickly. For example, you might use a blue highlighter to mark important dates and names, a green one for definitions, and a yellow one for formulas. Regardless of your color code, it will help you focus on specific information during test review sessions.

There is nothing special about any particular system of coding. Some people put circles around definitions and boxes around formulas using a plain pen. Experiment with a system until you find one that works best for you, and then stick with it.

Fill in the left-hand column of your notes with key words and phrases. Review your class notes to identify the major ideas and their supporting points. When you have identified a key idea, select a word or phrase that describes it and place it next to that material on the left-hand side of the vertical line you drew earlier. For example:

Final battle of Am. Revolution	Yorktown, VA, was the site of the final surrender of British forces that ended the American Revolutionary War

Conduct a weekly review session for each class. In addition to your after-class review of your notes, you should schedule a 20- to 30-minute weekly review session for each class in which you review the cleaned-up version of your notes. A good time to do this is on a weekend. During this review, the value of the Cornell note-taking system will become apparent to you.

When you begin your weekly review, take your class notes for the week out of your three-ring binder and arrange them in reverse order so that the first page is on the bottom of the pile and the last page is on the top. Fan the pages out so that all you can see on each page is the left-hand column, and then set them down. Now you are ready to begin your review. For each exposed key word and phrase in the left-hand column, try to recall the corresponding entry in the right-hand column. Check your answer by raising the sheets covering the right-hand column.

If you have coded your notes as suggested before, look now for all the items with the same code. For example, if you want to review just definitions, look for all these coded items. Next, you might want to look at your coded formulas. Continue until you have reviewed all the material from that week's class. You may want to take this approach further and use the weekly review session to develop 3" x 5" flash cards of the key terms, definitions, dates, and so on. Place the term or word on one side of the card and the answer on the other. Then carry these with you and review them whenever you have a few spare moments.

Develop mind maps from your notes. Mind mapping is another good way to enhance the review of your weekly class notes. It will help you put order to the new information you received during the week. We will discuss how to develop a mind map in Chapter 9.

Review your notes the day before the next class using key words and phrases. The day before the next class, look over your notes from the previous class for 10 to 20 minutes. Cover up the right-hand column and test your recall of what is there by looking at key words and phrases in the left-hand column. This will reinforce what you learned in the last class and help focus your mind on what the next class will cover.

With this approach to note taking, you can quickly and effectively review what you learned in class to get the most out of each class session. By the time the next test comes along, you will already understand the major points, their supporting arguments, their differences and similarities, any relevant formulas, and the key terminology. In essence, you will already be well prepared to take the next test. Since most of the necessary information is already on its way to your long-term memory, you can spend most of your test preparation time dealing with details. You will also discover that you can retrieve this information from memory for other tests, including the final examination. The biggest payoff is that your class notes are now an asset rather than a liability to your college success.

Exercise 4.1 *Rewrite a set of class notes immediately after completing a specific class. Write a brief analysis of the major differences between your original notes and your rewritten notes.*

_____

_____

_____

_____

_____

Exercise 4.2 *In groups of three or four students, exchange some class notes (ideally, these would all be from the same course). Discuss the strengths and weaknesses of the different sets of notes.*

Exercise 4.3 *Use the Cornell system of note taking in at least one of your classes. After each class session, identify the major topic of your notes. Then write down at least two new pieces of information that support that topic.*

Exercise 4.4 *Assume your notes contain some information that contradicts what you learned in high school. In groups of three or four students, discuss what approach you would use to verify the information in your notes. Discuss how you would share your feelings with your professor.*

Exercise 4.5 *Set up a page according to the Cornell note-taking system. Then, on the right-hand side of the page, write a paragraph describing the Cornell system, its advantages, and how you can use it in a college course. In the left-hand column, write down some key words taken from your paragraph.*

Exercise 4.6 *Choose one of your classes and take notes during a lecture. Also, make a tape-recording of the lecture. After class, listen to the recording and write down some notes. Then write a paragraph comparing the quality of the notes you took in class to the quality of the notes you took from the tape recording. Explain any differences you find.*

Exercise 4.7 *Simplify a set of lecture notes for a single class period by making 3" x 5" cards. Write a paragraph describing what you learned from this exercise and how you might use these cards.*

▲ Taking Notes in Your Textbook

You can apply the same note-taking system to reading assignments in your textbook. Start by skimming the material to get a feel for the big ideas and concepts. As they become apparent to you, write them in the left-hand margin of your textbook as you did with your class notes. (If the textbook is not yours to keep, write on a separate piece of paper.) You can also use in your textbook the same coding system you used in your class notes. Now read the material a second time and turn headings and subheadings in the book into questions. For example, if the subheading is "Elements of a Learning Style," change it to "What Are the Elements of a Learning Style?" Then, when you read the material a third time, you will actively look for the answers to those questions and highlight or mark them in some way.

If you follow the active learning approach presented in this chapter, you will increase your ability to get the most out of each class and to do well on your exams. The success of this approach depends on your commitment to active learning in every class. All-night cramming sessions will be a thing of the past as you replace them with many short study sessions in which you retain more of what you learn for a longer period of time.

Exercise 4.8 *Describe in a paragraph how one day's set of class notes relates to the entire course.*

Exercise 4.9 *In groups of three or four students, summarize one day's set of class notes from one course. Now compare your notes with those of the other group members. Share with group members three ways your notes are similar to theirs and three ways your notes differ. What did you learn from the other students' notes? Each group should be prepared to share their discussion with the rest of the class.*

Exercise 4.10 *Break up into pairs for a "pair and share" activity. Each pair will create ten questions pertaining to this class. Then exchange questions with another pair of students and quiz each other on those questions. On a separate piece of paper, write a brief paragraph summarizing how well your pair responded to the other pair's questions. What did you learn from this exercise?*

Exercise 4.11 *Using Bloom's taxonomy of the cognitive domain, construct questions related to your notes or the reading material from this course. Write at least one question reflecting each of the six levels of Bloom's taxonomy. (See Chapter 2, pages 26–27.)*

Exercise 4.12 *Using your notes from any one of your courses, write down the major ideas and any supporting information presented so far in that class. Share with the class the strengths and weaknesses of your notes. (It's a good idea to do this exercise again toward the end of the semester and then compare your analyses.)*

_____

_____

_____

_____

_____

Exercise 4.13 *Choose one of your classes and use the Cornell note-taking method for at least one week. Then set up an appointment with your professor to discuss your class notes. Have him or her check for accuracy, thoroughness, and comprehension of the major concepts. Ask your professor how you might improve your note taking for that class. Be prepared to share the details of your meeting with the rest of the class. (It would be a good idea to write a thank-you note to your professor for the time and assistance.)*

Exercise 4.14 *On a separate piece of paper, write a paragraph explaining how you might integrate a set of purchased class notes with your own class notes to enhance your overall course experience.*

CHAPTER HIGHLIGHTS

1. Since most of the material on college exams comes from what is presented in class, successful note taking is important to your college success.

2. A well-executed lecture can give you a false sense of security about your grasp of the material.

3. Good note taking means being an active learner, not just a scribe who writes down everything the professor says.

4. Before a class begins, complete all outside assignments, review your notes, find a seat near the front center of the classroom, and make sure you have all the necessary materials.

5. During class, constantly evaluate the material being presented. Use the Cornell note-taking style, write down all specific information, leave lots of white space in your notes, and mark all your notes with the date, page number, subject, and course name.

6. Use a separate three-ring binder for each course so you can put all the course materials together in one place.

7. Write only on one side of the paper so your notes will be easier to read and organize.

8. Listen for clues from your professors about what is important.

9. After class, review and clean up your notes within 24 hours to avoid forgetting the material.

10. After class, fill in the left-hand column of each page of notes with key words and phrases.

11. Conduct weekly review sessions for each class, and develop mind maps for each major topic.

12. Apply the classroom note-taking techniques to outside textbook readings.

CHAPTER HIGHLIGHTS

CASE STUDY

Franco's Frustration

Barry had finally had it! For an hour he had listened to his roommate mumble, groan, and throw things around his side of the room. "Franco, what is your problem?" Barry bellowed. "I have an English paper I'm trying to finish, and I can't even think with all the noise you're making. Tell me what's bothering you or go somewhere else."

Franco immediately saw that his frustration about tomorrow's chemistry test was really getting to him. He explained to Barry that this was his second chemistry test of the semester and he had no idea what was going on in the course. He had attended every class and written down everything the professor had said. He thought he knew what was going on because he could follow everything in class, but when he started studying for the test last night, he realized he did not understand *any*thing. His notes were useless. There were many parts he could not read, and what he could read made little sense. To make matters worse, he could not remember anything from the first test, which he had misplaced. His greatest fear was the comprehensive final exam he would have to take in just three weeks. He had studied the entire night before the first test, yet barely passed it. He also had two other tests earlier this week, which left him no time to study for the chemistry test until today.

Barry began to understand what Franco was going through as he watched him pick up the spiral-bound notebook that contained Franco's chemistry notes. When Franco threw it into the corner, all the loose papers he had stuffed into it went flying everywhere. Professor Krantz sure must have given out a lot of handouts in his class. At the bottom of the pile, Barry noticed Franco's chemistry book. When Franco calmed down, Barry asked him if the book was any good. Franco replied that he had looked at it a few times, but felt his professor was one of those who wanted only to hear his own words regurgitated back to him on the test. As a result, Franco had studied only the material covered in class. Besides, the guy talked so fast that keeping up was hard. Franco said he spent his whole class period writing as fast as he could before Professor Krantz erased it off the board. Everyone said Krantz was the most disorganized professor in the world. Anyone who went to his office would agree: You could hardly get the door open for all the papers strewn about. If only Franco had gotten one of the other professors who teach this course! They were much more organized and ran a smoother ship. Franco finished his venting by saying, "It's all Krantz's fault. If only I had registered for classes earlier, I could have gotten another professor and not been stuck with Krantz. Then this wouldn't be happening to me."

Do you agree or disagree with Franco? Explain your answer. What advice would you give to Franco? Be specific.

Personal Journal

SELF-AWARENESS

Personal Journal 4.1 Describe a time when your class notes caused you to do poorly on an exam. How did that make you feel? Describe a course where you did very well, and explain why you did well in that course. How did that make you feel? Based on what you have learned in this chapter, how will you change your approach to note taking? Be specific.

_____

_____

_____

_____

_____

_____

_____

_____

_____

DIVERSITY

Personal Journal 4.2 Suppose you have a classmate who is deaf and has college-provided tutors for every class. The tutors provide him with an excellent set of typed notes after each class. The student does very well on all the tests. How do you feel about the professional set of notes this student receives? Do you think this creates an unfair advantage? Or do you believe colleges should do even more to assist their deaf students?

_____

_____

_____

_____

_____

_____

_____

_____

_____

ETHICS

Personal Journal 4.3 Which of the following do you consider cheating? For the items you check, explain how and to what extent you think they constitute cheating.

❑ Borrowing your roommate's notes for a class you missed

❑ Purchasing notes prepared by a commercial business

❑ Using notes an interpreter has prepared to compensate for a disability

_____

_____

_____

_____

_____

_____

_____

_____

_____

ETHICS

Personal Journal 4.4 How does your school define cheating? What is your definition of cheating? In your opinion, what should be the consequences for a student caught cheating on a homework assignment? On a lab report? On a quiz? On a term paper? On a final exam?

_____

_____

_____

_____

_____

_____

_____

_____

_____

CHAPTER QUIZ

1. Explain why it is better to review your class notes daily than to wait until a few days before an exam.

   _____

   _____

   _____

   _____

   _____

2. Explain how completing outside assignments before class helps you take better notes.

   _____

   _____

   _____

   _____

3. Describe the Cornell style of note taking. What are its advantages? How does this system help you prepare for an exam?

_____

_____

_____

_____

_____

4. Explain why it is better to use a three-ring binder than a spiral-bound notebook for class notes.

_____

_____

_____

_____

_____

5. Why is it important to review your notes within 24 hours after class?

_____

_____

_____

_____

CHAPTER 5

Reading Skills

CHAPTER OBJECTIVES

After reading this chapter, you will understand why:

- Reading skill development strengthens your overall learning skills.
- Reading skills evolve over a lifetime.
- Intensive reading skills apply to reading in college.
- Effective reading reflects good problem-solving skills.

After reading this chapter, you will know how to:

- Identify and apply efficient reading strategies.
- Evaluate your reading comprehension.
- Assess your reading strengths and weaknesses using formative and summative evaluations.
- Set your long-term reading goals.

Good reading ability is an often overlooked skill but is critical to your college success. About 35 to 45 percent of your chance at graduating from college depends on how well you read. Reading assignments are your primary sources of information in most college courses. As much as 50 percent of many course exams are based on reading assignments not discussed in class. Your success on these exams depends on your ability to independently comprehend, interpret, and evaluate reading assignments. Both the quantity and the difficulty of the readings you undertake in college will far exceed those of most prior reading assignments. Typically, a college professor will assign 600 to 750 pages of reading per class per semester. Whatever your current reading level, you will need to pay greater attention to your reading assignments and assume more personal responsibility for your reading skills. You may need to develop some strategies to improve your reading skills and increase your comprehension.

In this chapter, you will find out how reading strengthens your ability to understand new and complex ideas. You will learn how to read more effectively so you can comprehend more. By enhancing your ability to synthesize, analyze, apply, and evaluate what you read, you will become a better critical thinker who can apply the higher-level thinking skills at the top of Bloom's taxonomy. In the end, you will commit new information to your long-term memory more quickly because you employed effective strategies to process what you read.

▲ Improving Your Reading Skills

As you develop more sophisticated reading skills, you will better understand and remember what you read. You will also become better at explaining what you have read on tests and in oral presentations. Along the way, you will increase your ability to compare and contrast the ideas of different authors. You will recognize cause-and-effect relationships and ultimately be able to make inferences, draw conclusions, construct generalizations, and evaluate reading selections. When this happens, you will be using all levels of the cognitive domain—understand, comprehend, apply, synthesize, and evaluate—as you read. In the previous chapters, you learned how to be an active learner; now you can be an active reader. An active reader improves comprehension through predicting, self-questioning, clarifying, and summarizing.

Thinking skills, writing skills, and reading skills are very much the same. For all of them, you use your brain to interpret numbers and words to express your thoughts or make sense of the ideas of others. Whether reading, writing, or thinking, you are engaged in an enormously active endeavor despite your quiet appearance.

Reading for the purpose of rote memorization reduces your comprehension of the material. On the other hand, if you connect new knowledge with previously known information, you may come up with important new concepts or ideas. You become a better student by applying your critical thinking skills to reading. You also enhance and strengthen your reading skills by having a positive attitude toward reading.

When bright students fail in college, the reason often is poor reading habits. Reading is a deliberate activity demanding your full attention and your personal commitment to increase your comprehension.

▲ The Role of Evaluation

Evaluation is an important part of your personal growth because it holds you accountable for what you do and gives you a chance to improve. The same is true for reading. Good readers evaluate what they read for these same two reasons. They want to be sure they fully understand what they have read, and they are looking for ways to improve their knowledge and reading skills. Professors assign large amounts of outside reading for similar reasons: to improve their students' knowledge and understanding of a topic. They hold their students accountable for reading these assignments by looking for how the material influences students' work.

Researchers often use two types of evaluation strategies: formative evaluation and summative evaluation. **Formative evaluation** occurs at intermittent stages in the development of an idea, a product, or a service. The purpose of this type of evaluation is systematic improvement. A **summative evaluation** is used to assess an idea, a product, or a service at the conclusion of an effort. When you finish this chapter, you will recognize how you can employ both forms of evaluation to improve your reading comprehension.

ACTIVE LEARNING

Exercise 5.1 *Take a look at all your reading assignments for the current semester (use your class syllabi). How many pages will you be expected to read by the end of the semester in each course? For all your courses? For each week of the semester? Describe in a few sentences your reading objectives for each course and how you plan to complete your reading assignments.*

_____

_____

_____

_____

_____

ACTIVE LEARNING

Exercise 5.2 *During your next reading session, time yourself to see how long you can read without stopping. Do this two more times, keeping a record of your time. Do you think your ability to read without stopping needs improvement? List three things you can do to increase your uninterrupted reading time.*

_____

_____

_____

_____

_____

▲ Developing Your Metacognition Skills

The effectiveness of your reading depends not only on your ability to understand and interpret each word you read but also on your ability to comprehend ideas. Simply recognizing words and main ideas may have been enough until now, but in college you need to comprehend much more. Being a successful college reader means you must be an efficient reader who maximizes what is learned from each reading session. There are four prerequisites to accomplishing this:

- You must have well-developed language skills.
- You must open your mind to new ideas.
- You must focus your mind fully on learning.
- You must devote your time and energy to getting the job done.

These prerequisites set the stage for effective reading and learning. Successful students work hard to meet all these prerequisites when they read.

Even when they meet these prerequisites, some students still do poorly because they fail to apply appropriate reading and thinking strategies to the reading and learning process. Meeting the prerequisites and knowing when and where to apply the strategies is what differentiates successful students from unsuccessful ones. Successful students know how to use their valuable metacognition skills.

Simply put, **metacognition** is understanding how people think. This chapter emphasizes how you can apply your metacognition skills (or your problem-solving skills) to college reading. First, you must learn to recognize some common strategies used by authors. Next, you need to develop ways to evaluate your own metacognition skills when you read. Finally, you must develop your ability to decide which strategies to use and know when and where to apply them. What strategies you choose depends to a large extent on how you process information.

RECOGNIZING ORGANIZATIONAL PATTERNS

Recognizing organizational patterns in your reading material is an important first step in developing your metacognition skills. You will want to be able to recognize and separate main ideas, supporting examples, and details. An author may arrange the material chronologically or explain data in formulas or charts. You also will want to look for contextual clues that show how the author uses patterns of comparisons or contrasts to get a point across. If you can figure out how the author puts the information together for the reader, you will improve your own reading comprehension.

Four commonly used organizational patterns are the following:

Enumeration	A list of dates, names, formulas, theories, and so on that the author believes is important to understanding the larger concept of the material
Time order	A list of the major events or sequence of events in the order they occur
Cause-effect	An explanation of how one thing causes other things to happen
Compare-contrast	An explanation of how events, discoveries, and so on are the same or different

Organizational patterns can also exist as internal or external patterns. An **external organizational pattern** is a visual presentation of the printed material. It might be the way the author arranges the table of contents, how the book is explained in the introduction, or how graphic representations are depicted. An **internal organizational pattern** is the specific point of view the author uses (eyewitness, advocate, analyst, and so on) to put together the information and ideas being communicated. Such a pattern might be found in the introduction, in the first chapter of the book, or in the first few paragraphs of a chapter.

ACTIVE LEARNING

Exercise 5.3 *Without looking back on what you have read so far, write a two-sentence description of the major point of this chapter. List the steps you used to remember the content. What organizational patterns (external and internal) were used?*

_____

_____

_____

_____

_____

COLLABORATIVE LEARNING

Exercise 5.4 *Break up into groups of three or four and delete any material in this chapter that your group thinks is unnecessary. Be prepared to discuss your group's rationale for deleting the information. Then compare what your group deleted with what the other groups deleted.*

▲ Comprehension Skill Tips

To apply reading and learning strategies effectively, you must first define the strategies you will use. Then you must determine when and where to use them. Research shows that students who know something about reading strategies do better in school. The following sections define several strategies to use before, during, and after reading and briefly explain how to use them in your reading assignments.

BEFORE YOU START TO READ

Strategy 1: *Know the purpose for each reading assignment and why you should be interested in this new knowledge.* Ask yourself, your professor, and other students about the purpose of the assigned reading. Then relate the general content to your own past experience by connecting it to prior knowledge. This procedure helps you identify the most important questions at issue before you start to read. It then follows that you will be looking for the answers to these questions as you read. You can expand this step by asking yourself what the author's purpose is throughout the assigned material. Be sure to apply formative questions rather than summative questions. By making connections to your past knowledge and to the important questions at issue, you construct your own sense of the meaning of the reading.

Strategy 2: *Skim the book's preface and table of contents to decide what organizational structure the author has chosen.* In the preface, authors often reveal their approach to the subject, their central themes, or their objectives for writing the text. The table of contents identifies the sequence of presentation and any organizational patterns.

Strategy 3: *Read the summary paragraphs at the end of each reading segment so you will know what the author thinks is important before you start reading.* Frequently authors state the main ideas plainly in summary form in the final few paragraphs of the chapter or text.

Strategy 4: *Identify lists of learning objectives at the beginning of each chapter or reading segment.* Active learners make these objectives into study questions to help them identify the important points in the reading. As you read, search for more detailed material about these objectives. Look for how the text structures or organizes ideas, and identify important sequences and patterns associated with the chapter or the entire book. Identify how the objectives relate to the various levels of Bloom's taxonomy so you will recognize the level of cognitive skill you are using. Ask yourself if you are just memorizing facts or understanding and relating broad concepts.

Strategy 5: *Read any study questions found at the end of the chapter or section so you know what the author thinks is important before you start reading.* Then, as you read, look for the answers to these questions and identify the major learning points of the material.

WHILE YOU ARE READING

Strategy 1: *Look for major headings and subheadings in the reading material.* Then turn the headings and subheadings into questions. For example, a heading titled "The Boston Tea Party" could be turned into "What is the importance of the Boston Tea Party?" As you read, look for the answers to your questions. Be sure your answers go beyond the facts to the critical thinking elements of understanding the text. This strategy helps you to recognize organizational patterns and increase your comprehension.

Strategy 2: *Examine the first few lines of each section of the text to identify the main ideas.* Sometimes authors state the main idea plainly in the first few sentences of each section; in other cases, authors infer it. Usually main ideas develop logically the important facts that are supported by minor facts and details. Once you discover the main ideas, you can start to identify the supporting ideas and arguments that relate to the major objective of the text. This strategy pinpoints the intended purposes of your reading.

Strategy 3: *Write a brief outline of the major ideas and supporting ideas as you read.* An outline helps you see, and thus understand, the author's main ideas. As you create an outline, relate what you are reading to other ideas you have on the subject or to your personal experiences. By making links to your prior knowledge, you will understand the material more easily. At this point, you can also sort the information into a framework you can easily retrieve from your long-term memory. Remember, reading is active work. It requires you to move backward and forward to enhance comprehension.

Strategy 4: *Read with a dictionary.* Misunderstanding the meaning of just one word can change the meaning of an entire paragraph. Context clues often hint at what words mean. If you do not have a dictionary at hand, write down the unfamiliar words in a notebook and look them up later. But first, exercise your brain and predict what an unknown word might mean. Reread the paragraph or the page, or move forward to figure out the meaning of the word. Make a list of all new words that need clarification for you to fully understand the reading.

Strategy 5: *Look for bold print that may indicate important words, formulas, definitions, charts, or graphs.* This helps you identify new words and main ideas, which in turn will lead you to the major and supporting points.

Strategy 6: *Focus!* Do your reading someplace where you can focus completely on what you are reading. College textbook reading is very different from reading a novel for pleasure. You may have to read an assignment several times to understand its full meaning. It is a good idea to read your assignment three times. First, skim the material to get an overview and discover the author's organizational patterns. Second, read for content using the reading strategies above. Third, read the assignment one more time to find good answers to all your questions and to improve your comprehension.

Strategy 7: *Predict information in the reading selection.* **Anticipate** *the outcomes or the content to engage yourself in the reading/thinking process.*

AFTER YOU READ

Strategy 1: *After you have read the assignment,* **review** *the material to find the answers to all the questions you developed by using the preceding strategies.* Then create a summative evaluation of what you have read and test your overall understanding of the reading selection.

Strategy 2: *Explain what you read out loud to yourself, another student, or a small study group.* This gives you an opportunity to verbally summarize your understanding of the content and to make a summative evaluation of the reading. If you do your summary in a small study group, encourage the other students to describe their understanding of the material and what strategies they used so you can improve your own comprehension.

Exercise 5.5 *On a separate piece of paper, write a short summative evaluation as it relates to the organization of one of your course textbooks. What are three strengths of the text you are evaluating? What are three weaknesses of that text?*

Exercise 5.6 *Describe in one paragraph why the author of the textbook you used in Exercise 5.5 is an expert. How did you assess the text? Pair up with another student in your class and explain the strategies you used to assess the text you chose. Then ask your partner to assess your thinking process.*

▲ Developing Your Monitoring Strategies

To measure your progress in reading and learning, you will need to develop some monitoring strategies. It is important to continually evaluate your metacognition skills. First, you must decide what abilities you will measure to evaluate how you are doing.

You should evaluate your ability to

- Determine the reading difficulty of a reading selection
- Recognize patterns in the reading selection
- Make connections to your prior knowledge and information
- Know how relevant information relates to the goals of the entire reading selection
- Rank the value of the selection
- Recognize contradictions with other things you have read or with your personal beliefs
- Determine how open-minded you are about the information
- Judge your reaction to the content of the text (Do you agree or disagree? Were you surprised, amused, or angry?)
- Use clues to move backward and forward in the text to discover greater meaning
- Be flexible in monitoring your comprehension of the material

▲ Developing Your Comprehension Strategies

As you monitor your comprehension, you will want to develop some strategies to help you increase your understanding of the reading material. Some specific comprehension strategies include summarization, mental imagery, story grammar, mnemonic imagery, question generation, and prior knowledge activation. Remember, you can use more than one strategy to evaluate your comprehension.

Strategy 1: *Summarization.* As you summarize the main points and subpoints of a passage, you will be able to eliminate trivial or redundant information. Here are some ways to summarize the information:

- Identify the topic sentence for each paragraph.
- Outline the text using major headings and subheadings.
- Draw graphics to illustrate the information.
- Make a list of problems that need to be resolved (include actions needed to resolve them).

Strategy 2: *Mental imagery.* If facts are confusing or obscure, try constructing mental images, or picturing them in another way. For example, you might visualize a set of complicated chemical reactions as a computer game in which the next step in the sequence is another level of the game. Sometimes the weirdest images are the easiest to remember, so be creative.

Strategy 3: *Story grammar.* Try turning your reading material into a story. Ask questions about the passage as though it were a story:

- Who is the main character?
- Where and when does the story take place?
- What do the characters do?
- How does the story end?
- How do the main characters feel?

Questions like these will help you recall important details and improve your understanding and comprehension of the text in an enjoyable way.

Strategy 4: *Mnemonic imagery.* Mnemonic imagery translates words or ideas into a form that will trigger your memory. That form might be an acrostic, a picture, or a graph. A good example of mnemonic imagery is the acrostic "HOMES" often used to remember the names of the Great Lakes: Huron, Ontario, Michigan, Erie, and Superior.

Strategy 5: *Question generation.* As you read a selection, generate questions that require you to think about the meaning of the passage.

Strategy 6: *Prior knowledge activation.* As you read, relate what you already know to the information in the passage. Then predict how you think this information will evolve in the text.

COMMON ELEMENTS OF IMPROVED READING COMPREHENSION

Whatever strategies you choose to evaluate your comprehension, there are four common themes throughout:

- Predict
- Self-question
- Clarify
- Summarize

In other words, be an active reader. If you utilize these four themes as you read, you will probably see the greatest increase in your reading comprehension. Although arranged differently, these four themes are important elements of the following six popular reading techniques:

SQ3R	survey, question, read, review, recite
PQ4R	preview, question, read, reflect, recite, review
PQRST	preview, question, read, state, test
Triple S	scan, search, summarize
OK5R	overview, key idea, read, record, recite, review, reflect
OARWET	overview, achieve, read, write, evaluate, test

These different combinations of reading strategies emphasize the need for students to be familiar with many strategies to improve their reading comprehension. Clearly there is no one "right" way to be an effective reader, nor is there only one way to organize a reading plan. In fact, each strategy involves many activities. The steps in each method are similar, and together they make up effective comprehension strategies.

An integral part of metacognition strategies includes dynamic interactions between students and professors in the classroom. But when you read, you decide your own reading rate, your focus, your comprehension strategies, your monitoring methods, your problem-solving techniques, and your criteria for evaluation. Good readers are active readers. As they read, they constantly use the right strategies to produce the best results.

▲ Improving Your Reading Skills

Most students generally know how well they read. Unfortunately, many rate reading as their worst student skill. As you found at the start of this chapter, good reading skills are a vital ingredient in getting your college diploma. But if reading has never been "your thing," what can you do? The answer is simple: The more you read, the better a reader you will become. Increased reading enhances your reading skill and improves your reading competence. *It is never too late to become a good reader!* If reading is not one of your strengths, seek out help. Reading is too important to your college success to ignore it. Improvement in reading alone can make the rest of your courses more rewarding. Most schools offer confidential, low-cost, or free reading help because they recognize how vital reading is for achieving one's life goals.

It is helpful to know how to determine the reading level of your material. Several popular methods are available to help you calculate reading levels. One is the **Fog Reading Index**, which suggests the following procedure to determine the reading level of a passage:

1. Select a reading sample of 100 words.

2. Count the number of sentences within the sample.

3. Divide the 100-word sample by the number of sentences.

4. Count the number of hard words by counting the number of words with three syllables or more. Do not count proper nouns, compound ready words, or verb forms made into three syllables.

5. Add together the numbers calculated in steps 3 and 4.

6. Multiply the total number from step 5 by .4 to identify the approximate grade level.

COLLABORATIVE LEARNING

Exercise 5.7 *Determine the reading levels of four different sections of this text by using the Fog Reading Index. Compare any differences in the reading levels. Then compare your answers with those of other class members. Now do the same thing for a textbook from one of your other courses this semester. In groups of three or four, compare and contrast the different textbooks reviewed by the other students in your group.*

Once you have determined the reading level of a passage, you will want to find out if you are prepared to read that material. The **Cloze Procedure** gives you insight into how well prepared you are to read a particular text. It also evaluates your reading comprehension. To complete a Cloze Procedure, you make inferences based on your grammatical knowledge. Certain words are deleted in a reading selection, and you are asked to use context clues to predict the missing words. The standard deletion rate is every fifth word in a passage of 200 words. The answers are considered correct if the exact word is chosen or a synonym fits the context. The cut-off score for an acceptable performance is 40 percent.

Another reading assessment tool is the **Nelson-Denny Reading Test**, a standardized test that measures reading comprehension at the college level. This test includes two subtests: vocabulary and reading comprehension. The vocabulary section consists of 100 multiple-choice items. The comprehension test consists of eight passages followed by 36 multiple-choice questions. The first minute of the test is used to determine your reading rate.

The **Index of Reading Awareness (IRA)** is a reading assessment tool that provides valuable questions for readers to ask themselves. The IRA focuses on measuring evaluation, planning, regulation of the reading process, and adjusting reading strategies while monitoring reading progress. The IRA serves as a self-questioning tool to determine reading progress by asking the following questions:

1. What is the hardest part about reading for you?

2. What would help you become a better reader?

3. What is special about the first sentence in a chapter of a textbook?

4. How are the last sentences in a chapter special?

5. If you could read only some sentences of a chapter because you were in a hurry, which ones would you read?

6. When you tell other people about what you are reading, what do you say?

7. If your professor told you to read a chapter of a textbook to remember the general meaning, what would you do?

8. Before you start to read, what kind of plans do you make to help you read better?

9. If you had to read very fast and could read only some words, which ones would you try to read?

10. What would help you read faster?

11. Why do you go back and read things again?

12. What do you do if you come to a word and you do not know what it means?

13. What do you do if you do not know what a whole sentence means?

14. What parts of a chapter do you skip as you read?

15. If you were reading a text for recreation, what would you do?

16. If you were reading for a science class, what would you do to remember the information?

17. If you were reading for a test, what would help you the most?

18. If you were reading a book to write a report, what would help you the most?

19. What is the best way to remember a chapter of a textbook?

20. What statement best defines the main idea of a text?

ACTIVE LEARNING

Exercise 5.8 *Using a table like that in Figure 5.1, fill in the names of five of your college courses in the left-hand column. (If you do not have five courses, fill in as many as you have.) For each course, answer questions 3, 4, 6, 8, 14, and 18 from the Index of Reading Awareness. Summarize your findings in a brief paragraph.*

_____

_____

_____

_____

_____

FIGURE 5.1 Index of Reading Awareness (IRA)

Course	Answer to Question 3	Answer to Question 4	Answer to Question 6	Answer to Question 8	Answer to Question 14	Answer to Question 18
1.						
2.						
3.						
4.						
5.						

▲ *Establishing Goals for Improving Reading Skills*

To establish goals for improving your reading skills, you will need to know some things about your present reading skills. The Reading Inventory in Exercise 5.9 will help you evaluate your skills.

ACTIVE LEARNING

Exercise 5.9 *Take the Reading Inventory using the form in Figure 5.2. When you are finished, develop a summative evaluation of your reading skills and devise a written plan to improve them.*

_____

_____

_____

_____

_____

_____

FIGURE 5.2 **Reading Inventory**

Reading Factors:	Strong	Weak	Absent	Not Sure	Action Plan*
Reading rate					
Reading quantity					
Reading difficulty					
Delete unnecessary information					
Identify reading strategies					
Use self-questioning techniques					
Find topic sentences					
Read daily newspapers					
Visualize text					
Understand well					
Able to explain what I read					
Don't look back as I read					

Reading Factors:	Strong	Weak	Absent	Not Sure	Action Plan*
Look at titles, headings, and pictures					
Put information in my own words					
Reread					
Suspend judgment					
Open-minded					
Responsible					
Motivated					
Summarize					
Recognize patterns					
Other: _____					

*Suggested words to use in your action plans:

Reread	Guess meaning	Decide what I already know
Change reading rate	Visualize concepts	Outline the passage
Suspend judgment	Mark key points	Read beginning and end of passage first
Change attitude	Construct concept maps	Try again when I fail
Find new strategy	Write notes when reading	
Speak out loud about content	Skim for main ideas	

CHAPTER HIGHLIGHTS

1. Good reading skills are critical to college success.

2. Skimming reading assignments to get only the major points is not enough for college-level reading.

3. College reading requires comprehension, not just the acquisition of facts.

4. Good readers use a solid reading strategy that involves predicting, questioning, clarifying, and summarizing.

5. It is never too late to become a good reader.

6. Being a good reader leads to becoming an efficient learner, getting more out of each course, and achieving better grades.

CASE STUDY

Amy's Big Surprise

Amy began her first year of college with the confidence anyone would expect from a high school class valedictorian. When she was in elementary school, her teachers asked her to tutor some weaker readers, and in the ninth grade she was asked to read in some church services. She never thought for a moment that her reading was anything but outstanding. Of course, her family, teachers, guidance counselors, and high school principal were extremely optimistic about her college career as a chemistry major. She believed there was nothing to worry about as she looked forward to her fall semester at an outstanding four-year public university.

When Amy scheduled her college placement tests, she expected them to be less than challenging since her high school grades and SAT scores were very good. She had no doubts that her placement test results would be exemplary. However, the results took her and her parents by surprise. They showed that Amy qualified for beginning freshman composition as well as introductory calculus and chemistry. What caught her off guard was that her test scores were in the middle of those of all the other entering freshman students. Her college academic adviser explained that Amy could no longer compare herself with her former high school peers because she was now in a pool of similar students who were also very successful high school students.

During the first week of classes, Amy was overwhelmed by the size of the campus, the size of her classes, the cost of textbooks, and the amount of required reading assignments in each of her five courses. In the first week, she had a total of 375 pages of assigned reading. In addition, she was surprised to learn that she could not apply for her major until the end of her sophomore year. Admission to the university and to the major required two different evaluations. Entrance to the major was based solely on earning at least a 3.00 GPA in specific math, chemistry, biology, and English courses. In addition, by the end of her sophomore year, she had to be academically qualified to become a chemistry major. Her high school achievements, including her high school grades and SAT scores, were no longer relevant for admission to her chosen major.

At the end of freshman year, Amy had only a 2.5 GPA in her required courses. The courses were hard, but she thought she had done well enough to be accepted as a chemistry major. Now she just felt too stupid to pursue her dream of being a chemist. She was embarrassed because she did not measure up to her former teachers' and her family's expectations, and most of all she had failed to meet her own expectations.

Where did Amy go wrong? How should she assess her academic performance?

Personal Journal

SELF-AWARENESS

Personal Journal 5.1 Based on what you learned in this chapter, how would you rate your reading skills at this time? Do you think they are adequate for college? Explain your answer. Outline a plan to improve your reading skills.

_____

_____

_____

_____

_____

_____

_____

_____

SELF-AWARENESS

Personal Journal 5.2 What was the greatest book you ever read? Explain why you enjoyed reading it. How did you feel while you were reading it? How would you describe the quality of the writing? Would you read it again? Why or why not?

_____

_____

_____

_____

_____

_____

_____

_____

CRITICAL THINKING

Personal Journal 5.3 Analyze how the introduction to this textbook contributes to your learning the information in chapters 1 through 5.

_____

_____

_____

_____

_____

_____

_____

_____

_____

CHAPTER QUIZ

1. What does *metacognition* mean?

_____

_____

_____

_____

_____

2. Identify four reading strategies that are important to becoming a successful reader.

_____

_____

_____

_____

_____

3. Explain how you can use Bloom's taxonomy of the cognitive domain to become a better reader and learner.

_____

_____

_____

_____

4. What is the major difference between summative and formative evaluation?

_____

_____

_____

_____

5. Define the concept of readability and how it applies to this textbook.

_____

_____

_____

_____

ADDITIONAL RESOURCES

Chesla, E. *Reading Success: In 20 Minutes a Day.* 2nd ed. Ayer, Mass: Learning Express, 1998.

Dupuis, M. "The Cloze Procedure." *Journal of Educational Research*, 74(1), 1980, pp. 27–33.

Flemming, L. *Reading for Results.* Boston: Houghton Mifflin, 1999.

Kanar, C. *Becoming a Confident Reader.* Boston: Houghton Mifflin, 2000.

Kanar, C. *The Confident Reader.* Boston: Houghton Mifflin, 2000.

Kolb, D. A. *A Learning Style Inventory.* Philadelphia: McBer, 1985.

Maker, J. *Academic Reading with Active Critical Thinking.* Belmont, CA: Wadsworth, 2000.

Pressley, M. *Cognition, Teaching and Assessment.* New York: Longman, 1995.

Schaffzin, N. R. "Reading Smart: Advanced Techniques for Improved Reading." *The Princeton Review*, August 1994.

CHAPTER **6**

Test-Taking Skills

After reading this chapter, you will understand why:

- Success is a matter of positive attitudes and thorough preparation.
- A personal commitment to success brings success on tests.
- As your test scores improve, so will your confidence about test taking.
- Positive goals are the only acceptable goals.
- Being realistic about the importance of any single test can take the pressure off.
- Keeping your life goals flexible is important.
- Long-term learning is best accomplished with many short study sessions.

After reading this chapter, you will know how to:

- Develop a realistic, positive attitude toward tests.
- Prepare before a test.
- Determine what you need to do during the test to do well.
- Approach different types of tests.
- Handle different types of test questions.

Success is largely a matter of having a positive attitude and being thoroughly prepared. People who expect success and prepare for it are more likely to achieve their goals than those who do not. This also applies to success on tests. If you look at the people who do well on tests, you will find that most have positive expectations and work hard to prepare for tests.

There are many stories of students who flunked a course but returned later to retake it and received an *A*. When asked why things worked out so much better the second time around, these students say something like "I am not any smarter than I was the first time I took the course. However, I am much more serious about doing well in school and much better organized than I was back then." Attitude, preparation, and perseverance are worth at least as much as brainpower when it comes to success on tests.

Simply throwing up your hands and saying, "I just don't do well on tests" will not lead to real success. A negative attitude gives a test the power to control you and your ability to achieve. There may be times in your life, both in and out of school, when your future will depend on how you perform on a single test. It would be a shame if you could not practice law or medicine, or sell stock or insurance, because you could not pass the required state licensing exam. You do not want to waste years of school and hard work just because you "don't do well on tests."

You probably have a driver's license that required you to pass both a written and a performance test. Somehow you figured out a way to do well on that test because you really wanted to get a driver's license. You made a personal commitment to accomplish this, and you succeeded. If you make that same level of personal commitment to do well on tests in your college courses, you should succeed there too. All you need is a realistic, positive attitude, a firm commitment to success, and thorough test preparation.

This chapter aims to help you develop a positive attitude toward tests and to show you some simple preparation techniques that will improve your test performance. The combination of positive attitude and thorough preparation will increase your confidence. Success will breed success. As you gain control of this aspect of your life, tests will no longer govern your progress toward completing your life goals. You may even begin to look forward to future tests!

ACTIVE LEARNING

Exercise 6.1 *In a short essay, describe a time when you did well on an important test. What things made you do well on that test? How did you feel about yourself after you found out you did well on the test? What lessons did you learn from this experience?*

ACTIVE LEARNING

Exercise 6.2 *Describe how you prepared for your last big test. How did you do on that test? What could you have done differently to prepare for it? How will you prepare differently for the next test in that course?*

_____

_____

_____

_____

_____

▲ Developing a Positive Attitude Toward Tests

The first step in taking control of tests is to develop a proper attitude. A good attitude starts with establishing positive goals in all aspects of your life, including test taking. The proper goal for taking a test is: "I will do well on this test!" Negative goals such as "I must not fail this test" are not acceptable. Positive goals will help you focus your attention in the right direction and will lead you to the appropriate actions. By having positive goals, your mind thinks about achieving good things rather than avoiding bad things. Then, when positive things happen, such as a good test grade, you will have a feeling of accomplishment and progress. Focus on what you have done rather than on what you have left undone.

THE IMPORTANCE OF A SINGLE TEST

A good attitude also means being realistic about the importance of any given test. A single test grade should not ruin your life or lower your value as a person. Your grade reflects only how well you did on a test in a particular subject on a certain day. A poor grade on an introductory chemistry exam does not mean you have no future as a chemist any more than an A+ means you are destined to receive the Nobel Prize in Chemistry someday. It is just a test.

Do not put excessive or unrealistic pressure on yourself for any single test. Keep things in perspective. Imagine the worst thing that could happen if you failed this test, and then ask yourself if you could live with that outcome. If you can, you will face a lot less pressure. Now you can shift all the energy you would have spent worrying about failing the test to seeing to it that you do well.

Realistic, positive goals are the best goals because they leave you little time to worry about "something bad" happening. With this approach, even if something bad does happen, you are prepared to handle it. It is a setback rather than the end of the world. You just regroup and go on.

ALLOW FOR CHANGES

Despite a positive attitude and a lot of planning, very few people move forward in a straight line toward their life goals. Most experience a variety of dead ends, failures, and changes of direction in their lives. These experiences are natural parts of life and should be expected. Setbacks, failures, and changes are ways in which we learn and grow.

College is one of the best places to grow and test your life goals. As you gather new information about the world and about yourself, you may want to adjust your goals. Many students start college with a clear career objective in mind only to find themselves headed off in an entirely different direction after discovering a new part of life that they never knew existed. These new discoveries are what makes college such a critical part of your personal growth. Allowing your goals to expand and change is a key part of your lifelong self-discovery process.

Exercise 6.3 *On a separate piece of paper, develop a mind map for the major objectives of one of your courses. Use a time line, an acrostic, a graph, a chart, a picture, or some other device to depict these objectives. Then write a paragraph describing what you learned about the course material from your mind map.*

Exercise 6.4 *Develop a list of materials (pens, pencils, calculators, etc.) that you need to bring with you to your next test. Then list the things you can do to create a positive attitude about this test.*

_____

_____

_____

_____

_____

Exercise 6.5 *You have just received your first college test results in biology. Your score is below 50 percent. Describe a plan detailing what you will do to improve results on future tests.*

_____

_____

_____

_____

_____

Exercise 6.6 *You studied all night for a test and still did poorly. List three possible reasons for your poor performance. Then develop a written plan to prepare yourself for the next exam.*

_____

_____

_____

_____

_____

Exercise 6.7 *Discuss with one of your professors a particular test you have taken in that course. Construct five specific questions about how your instructor evaluates a student's final grade in the course. Write a summary of the major points of the interview. Report your findings to the class and share any unanswered questions you still have about how you will be evaluated in that course.*

▲ Preparing for a Test

Once you have developed a realistic, positive attitude toward tests, you can apply all your optimism to thoroughly prepare for your next test. Success requires both optimism and hard work.

BEFORE THE TEST

Use the Semester-at-a-Glance Calendar Getting ready for your first test of the semester starts on the first day of class. The first thing you should do is develop a semester-at-a-glance calendar, discussed in Chapter 3 (see pages 50–52). This calendar has a box for each day of the month and displays an entire month on one sheet of paper. Ideally, your calendar should display the whole semester on one page. Try taping together several sheets of paper to accomplish this. Be sure you hang up your semester-at-a-glance calendar on the wall of your official study area so you can see it every day. Also, carry a copy of it in your notebook or date book. On your calendar, enter every test date, final exam date, research paper due date, and other major assignment dates. Most professors list these dates in the course syllabus that they give out at the beginning of the semester.

With this system, you will never be surprised late on a Sunday night to find out that you have three exams in the next two days. Instead, you can start your preparation early enough to be thoroughly prepared for your exams and do well on all of them.

Review Class Material Daily The best way to start preparing for an exam is to review each subject for 20 minutes before and 20 minutes after every class session. In the before-class review, you will focus your thoughts on the upcoming class. You should review the reading or the problem assigned for that class period, formulate any questions from those assignments, and review your notes from the previous class. In the after-class review, you should look at your class notes, clarify what you wrote down, formulate questions for the next class, and skim the assignment for the next class.

These two 20-minute sessions will allow your brain to absorb the class material in small bits and digest it slowly. This "pickling period" increases the likelihood that the information will move from your short-term memory, where you often quickly forget it, to your long-term memory, where it is likely to stay. This approach is particularly important in courses in which the information builds on itself, such as math and science, and in courses that have comprehensive final examinations.

Review Course Material Weekly To supplement the daily course review sessions, you should schedule a one-hour, in-depth review of each course every week. Whereas the objective of the daily class review sessions is to master the details of the course, you conduct the weekly review to get an idea of the major themes, concepts, and ideas presented. Understanding these items will help you see how all the ideas in the course relate to one another. Mind mapping the course is one interesting way to conduct your weekly reviews.

The daily and weekly reviews will give you the "big picture" of the course, as well as most of the details (formulas, definitions, theories, and so on). During the week before an exam, you can focus on refining these ideas and their relationships so you can get full credit on all your answers and earn an *A* on the exam.

Exercise 6.8 *Organize a small study group, preferably among the members of this class. Develop a list of group rules related to meeting times, length of study group sessions, location of the sessions, and frequency of meetings. Also, identify a plan for reviewing the content being studied. Write a summary so all group members know what they have agreed to.*

ETHICS

Exercise 6.9 *Imagine that a study group member brings a copy of an upcoming test to a group meeting. In a one-page report, identify the ethical issues in this situation and describe what you would do and what the group should do. Be prepared to share your conclusions with the rest of the class.*

Exercise 6.10 *Evaluate a test you took recently and determine to what extent the test related to (1) the information covered in class, (2) the reading assignments given so far, and (3) class discussions up to this point. Write at least a one-paragraph summary of your conclusions.*

Exercise 6.11 *Create a plan describing how you would prepare for a test that is entirely made up of essay questions. Create a preparation plan for a test that is all true/false, multiple-choice, and short-answer questions.*

Exercise 6.12 *In a small study group, discuss how you might anticipate what the essay questions will be for an upcoming test. Write down some essay questions that you think might be on the test. Summarize the group's findings in writing. Be prepared to share them with the class.*

Exercise 6.13 *Assume that in one of your classes, you are assigned to a study group that is to write a paper on a specific topic. Your group has five members. Two members miss half of the group meetings. However, their names are included on the final group paper, and each member of the group will get the same grade. How does this make you feel? What should you do, if anything? Summarize in writing your group's plan to ensure that all students participate equally in the next group assignment. Discuss your plan with your group or with the entire class.*

THE WEEK BEFORE THE TEST

One week before a test, you should start the final phase of your test preparation. Your study sessions for this test may stretch to two or three hours per day.

Make a Checklist Your first step is to develop a checklist of everything you need to study. Your checklist might include the following:

- ❑ Definitions
- ❑ Theories
- ❑ Formulas
- ❑ Equations
- ❑ Types of problems
- ❑ Other important material

Then gather all the material in the categories you chose. You might find the information in the glossary or index of your textbook, in your class notes, or in your reading assignments. You may want to write down important information on 3" × 5" cards with the answer, definition, or formula on the back. Use these as flash cards. Be sure to carry them with you, and review them every time you have a few spare moments.

Ask the Professor It seems obvious that you should ask questions of your professor, but students often overlook this valuable source of information about the exam. Most professors are more than willing to tell you about the composition of the test (how the test is made up of essays, true-false, multiple-choice, or short-answer questions) and how long the test will take. If you listen carefully in class, especially the week before the test, you may find that the instructor gives hints about what is on the exam, such as "This is important" or even "This will be on the test." Be sure to verify what material and assignments the test will cover.

Get Copies of Old Exams Ask your instructor for copies of exams from previous years. Take one of these exams as if it were the real test. Most professors have adopted a preferred testing style; by taking an old exam, you will become comfortable with that style.

Make Up Your Own Examination If you have reviewed the course material thoroughly, you should have a good idea of what is important in the course. Now make up your own examination and write out the answers. The potential exam questions might come from any number of the following sources:

- ❏ Homework
- ❏ End-of-chapter questions
- ❏ Quizzes
- ❏ Examples from the textbook
- ❏ Class assignments

Another good source for potential exam questions is to turn the headings in your textbook into questions. For example, if the heading says "Factors Causing the Start of the American Civil War," turn it around to read, "What are the factors that caused the start of the American Civil War?" Your objective in making a mock exam is to thoroughly prepare yourself to answer just about any question your professor could ask from the course material. When you see similar questions on the test, your immediate response will be: I know the answer to that question, and I already answered it on my sample test. Each time you respond that way to a question, your grade will go up, and so will your test-taking confidence and your sense of subject mastery. You will then be in control.

THE DAY BEFORE THE TEST

Since you have been following a careful process to get ready for the test, you can now approach the day before the test with calmness. On that day, spend about one to three hours in a comprehensive review session in which you look over all the things you have done up until now. The objective of this session is to be sure you keep all the material fresh in your mind.

At the end of your last review session, make sure you have all the materials you will need to bring to the exam. These items might include the following:

- ❏ Watch
- ❏ Calculator
- ❏ Fresh batteries for calculator
- ❏ Pens
- ❏ Pencils
- ❏ Ruler
- ❏ Erasers
- ❏ Compass
- ❏ Other things you are allowed to bring with you

Verify the Time and Place of the Test Make sure you know the time and place of the test. If the test is a regular exam given as part of a course, it most likely will take place during a normal class period in the usual place. Do not forget that some large introductory classes have common exams that are sometimes held in the evening. Most final exams are held at times and places given by the university registrar. Be sure to check out this information well before you leave for the test. Now all you have left to do before the exam is to get proper rest, eat sensibly, and wear comfortable clothing to the exam.

DURING THE TEST

Arrive Early You should arrive 15 to 30 minutes before the exam is scheduled to start and confirm that you are in the right place at the right time. Arriving early should also give you a choice of seats; for example, you may prefer an aisle seat or a seat in the front center. If you are left-handed, you might want to get a left-handed desk. Most important, arriving early gives you time to relax before the test starts.

Write Down Formulas, Equations, Definitions, or Anything You Might Need During the Test As soon as you get your test paper, write down in the margins any important information you may be likely to forget.

Write Your Name on the Examination Be sure to write your name and any identification numbers on your test paper. This seems simple, but if the class is large and there are three or four papers without names, your professor will probably be unable to identify who wrote which test. This is particularly important on final examinations, when students leave the campus right after the exam.

Read the Entire Exam and Each Question Carefully Before Beginning A quick overview of the entire exam will give you a feel for the type of test you are facing. You will know if it is the kind of exam you expected. Sometimes information needed to answer earlier questions can be found in later questions on the same exam. Reviewing the entire exam will alert you to this information. If you have prepared properly, you should experience few surprises and feel confident that you will correctly answer each question.

Allocate Your Time According to Points If 10 percent of the points come from one question, you should allocate 10 percent of your time to that question. Investing 90 percent of your time to ensure getting full credit on a question worth 10 percent of the total points is not wise. You may end up without enough time to answer the other questions and fail the exam.

For example, suppose that in a 50-minute exam, three essay questions are given equal weight in the grading. The best way to allocate your time is to give each question no more than 15 minutes and allow 5 minutes for review and wrap-up. This is why it is important to bring a watch to the exam.

Make a Test-Answering Plan Now that you have reviewed the entire exam and allocated your time, you can make a plan to answer the questions. Simply put, you need to decide the order in which you will answer the questions. Usually it is best to start with questions that are short and easy to answer. Often these are short-answer, fill-in-the-blank, or true-false questions. Once you have targeted these questions, answer only the ones for which you know the right answer. You can come back to the other questions later if you have time. These types of questions are normally a small part of the overall points on a test.

How to Answer Questions There are four general types of test questions. Each type typically calls for a different approach to developing an answer.

Problem Usually problems are found on math and science tests, but they can appear on other tests as well. Be sure you read the entire problem carefully before starting your answer so you are sure you understand what kind of answer is needed. Always write out the complete formula for a calculation, since you will probably get at least partial credit even if you do not finish the problem or make a calculation error. Label your answer with the proper units. Circle your answer so the grader can find it easily. Move logically from step to step, and show your work. Evaluate your answer to see if it is reasonable. Ask yourself questions such as: Is the answer too big or too small given what was asked?

Short-Answer, Fill-in-the-Blank, and Matching These types of questions usually test your knowledge of definitions, formulas, theories, and simple facts. Drilling yourself with the flash cards you made earlier will ensure that you can answer these questions quickly and accurately. Skip the questions you do not know, since you may find information later in the test that will help you answer them.

Essay You must read essay questions carefully to ensure that you answer the question being asked. Develop an outline of your answer in the margin of the paper before you begin writing. It may help you gain at least partial credit if you do not have time to finish your answer, and it will help you put your points in logical order. Your theme or general hypothesis should be stated in the first few sentences. Devote the next few sentences to developing the evidence that supports your theme or hypothesis. How well you support your arguments is usually the key ingredient in getting full credit on an essay question.

An effective way to start your essay is to change the question to a statement. For example, if the question is "Why should business managers be interested in forecasting future business conditions?" change it to "Business managers should be interested in forecasting future business conditions for the following three reasons. . . . "

Underline the key words, terms, phrases, and findings in your essay so it will be easier for the grader to find them. Essays written in pen and on one side of the page are easier to read, so you are more likely to get more points. Leave room at the end of your essay to add to it if you have time. Read your essay before you turn it in to be sure it says what you intended.

Open-Book Test Open-book tests rarely offer students any advantages. If you have to look up everything in order to answer the questions, you probably will not have enough time to finish the exam. Before coming to the exam, mark important information in your book with Post-it® notes used as tabs. On your written notes, mark the pages that correspond to the information in your textbook so you can find things more easily. Condense your notes to one sheet of paper for each chapter or topic so you can quickly find the material the question requires.

If you come to the exam prepared for any type of question, you will be successful. Remember that test success is also the result of having a positive attitude and being thoroughly prepared. If you do both, you are unlikely to encounter any surprise questions on the test. As you read each question, you will say to yourself: I know how to answer that question. In most cases, you have either worked similar problems or already prepared an answer to that question.

If you apply the test strategies covered in this chapter, you will be transformed from a student who dreads tests to one who actually looks forward to them. You will control how well you do on tests and know how to effectively demonstrate what you have learned.

ACTIVE LEARNING

Exercise 6.14 *Would a poor test grade make you want to drop a course? Explain your answer. Describe the consequences of dropping one of your courses this semester. How might it affect your graduation?*

_____

_____

_____

_____

_____

ACTIVE LEARNING

Exercise 6.15 *You missed your final exam. You thought it was scheduled at 10:00 A.M. on Friday, but it was actually scheduled at 10:00 A.M. on Thursday. Explain what you would do.*

_____

_____

_____

_____

COLLABORATIVE LEARNING

Exercise 6.16 *Break up into groups of three or four and discuss the following scenario: In one of your classes, several students are collaborating on answering a take-home examination. The test was given as an individual rather than a group effort. The instructor does not know the students are cheating on the exam. In fact, the professor has a graduate student handling the exam. What problem does this situation create? (Be sure your group clearly defines the problem.) What people does this problem affect? Arrive at a consensus about what you should do, and report your conclusions to the class.*

CHAPTER HIGHLIGHTS

1. Doing well on a test, like many things in life, is a matter of having a positive attitude and being well prepared. Attitude, thorough preparation, and perseverance are worth at least as much as brainpower when it comes to taking a test.

2. Positive goals, such as "I will do well on this test," are the only acceptable goals. Negative goals, such as "I must not fail this test," are not acceptable. Positive goals focus you on achieving good things rather than on avoiding bad things.

3. Take your goals seriously and work hard to attain them. However, remember to keep your goals flexible as you learn more about yourself.

4. Successful test preparation requires thoroughness and many short study periods that start the first day of class.

5. Thorough test preparation makes you less likely to encounter any surprise questions. As you read each test question, you will realize that you know the answer because you worked a similar problem or prepared an answer to a similar question during your test preparation.

6. If you apply the test preparation strategies in this chapter, your test scores will increase, and you will become confident during tests. You may even start to look forward to them.

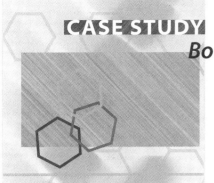

CASE STUDY
Bob's Big Blowout

Bob had a little extra bounce in his step as he headed down the hall to his freshman chemistry class. Today he would be getting back the first test in the course. Since this was also Bob's first test since coming to college, he was anxious to see how he did. Chemistry was one of his best subjects in high school, and that was a major reason he had decided to major in it. He knew he had to get an *A* in this course to be accepted into the major.

Bob was worried since the test had not gone as well as he had hoped. Because this course was so important to his future, he studied harder for this test than any he had ever taken. For three days before the test, Bob did nothing but study for it. In his excitement about the test, he almost missed it. On his way to the test, he ran into a friend who told him that he was headed in the wrong direction and then told him where the exam was being given. Bob arrived late for the exam, so he had to sit in the middle of a row rather than on an aisle, where he would have had some room to spread out. He no sooner sat down when the test began.

Bob was accustomed to answering test questions in order from first to last. The first question was tricky. He spent a lot of time on it before he got it right. Then he had to rush through the rest of the questions to get everything done in the time allotted. He was working on the last part of the final problem when the batteries in his calculator gave out. Fortunately, the rest of the exam was matching and true-false questions.

How well do you think Bob did on this test? Why? What should Bob have done differently to prepare for this test?

Personal Journal

Personal Journal 6.1 Select two courses that have tests in about two weeks and describe your plan to prepare for them. Include a time line that shows how you will study for these tests. Describe the most likely composition of the tests (essay, true-false, multiple-choice, etc.). Write a question and develop an answer for each type of question you expect to find on each test. How is this process different from the way you used to study for tests? How does creating your own questions prepare you for a test? How does this change your approach to test preparation?

_____

_____

_____

_____

_____

_____

_____

_____

Personal Journal 6.2 In light of what you have read in this chapter, why do you think some people do poorly on tests? What has been preventing you from doing your best on tests? Describe how you will change the way you prepare for a test.

_____

_____

_____

_____

_____

_____

_____

_____

_____

DIVERSITY

Personal Journal 6.3 Suppose there is a student in your class who is blind and has a tutor. The tutor takes notes for her and assists her during tests. This student is also given more time on tests than the others are. Write a short essay explaining whether you think it would be easier or more difficult to take a test orally with a tutor. What would be the advantages? What would be the disadvantages? Is extra test time an advantage in this situation? Do you think this student will get better grades because she has all this additional help? Explain why or why not.

_____

_____

_____

_____

_____

_____

_____

_____

CHAPTER QUIZ

1. Why are positive rather than negative goals the only acceptable goals?

_____

_____

_____

_____

_____

2. What are the advantages and disadvantages of pulling an "all-nighter" for an examination?

_____

_____

_____

_____

_____

3. List the steps you should take to prepare for a test.

_____

_____

_____

_____

_____

4. Why is long-term learning best accomplished with many short study sessions?

_____

_____

_____

_____

_____

CHAPTER 7

Writing Skills

CHAPTER OBJECTIVES

After reading this chapter, you will understand why:

- Good writing skills are an important part of your education.
- Having a keen sense of self-awareness and being an active learner are important in good writing.
- Writing is best thought of as a process.
- Clear thinking, time management, and hard work are important aspects of good writing.

After reading this chapter, you will know how to:

- Prepare a written assignment using a four-step writing method.
- Get started on a writing assignment.
- Develop a first draft.
- Transform prose to rhetoric.

One hallmark of a good college education is learning to write effectively. Your professors no doubt encourage you to develop this skill by requiring you to prepare many written reports and other papers. These assignments accomplish two objectives.

First, they provide a way to develop your critical thinking skills: your ability to understand, analyze, compare and contrast, draw conclusions, integrate new material into prior learning, and so on. In short, you must think well to write well.

Second, writing assignments give you an avenue for improving your general writing skills. Good writing skills are important not only to your success in college but also to your success in life. As you pursue a career, people will make important decisions that affect your future based solely on the quality of your written work. In fact, this may have already happened: You may have been admitted to college based solely on a written application and an essay. One study, reported in the December 17, 1998, issue of *Fortune* magazine, indicated that college graduates whose writing ability put them in the top quintile earned an average of three times more than those in the lowest quintile. Good writing skills do matter in life after college.

Unfortunately, most first-year college students admit that they dread writing assignments and that they do not think they are very good writers. But becoming good at anything requires constant practice. For example, if you want to run a marathon, you will do much better if you train hard for it. Similarly, you can also become a better writer by writing more. As you "train" to become a better writer, you will need to think clearly and you will require a plan. First, spend some time planning what you want to communicate, to whom you want to communicate, and how you want to communicate. Writing is like planting a garden: You need to do all the preliminary work of plowing, planting, fertilizing, and weeding before you get to harvest the crops. Good preliminary planning before you write lets you "harvest" your ideas into a good paper. There is no way you can shortcut this process and expect a good result.

Writing is one of the best ways to clarify your thoughts. Most people find it extremely satisfying to write down ideas and put them in a logical fashion that others can follow. This is not always an easy thing to do. You will need to have enough time to put your thoughts in good order before you can explain your ideas coherently in writing.

▲ The Value of Self-Awareness

A key ingredient in the development of clear thinking is a keen sense of self-awareness. Self-awareness gives you an objective view of yourself and a realistic perspective on how you interact with the world around you. Your personal journal is a good way to record your thoughts, reactions, and reflections of your world. Your journal entries show your personal growth and measure the development of your self-awareness. Each time you write in your journal, you understand more about yourself and how you perceive the world. Learning about yourself is a never-ending assignment, because you never stop changing and learning. An old expression says, "When you are through changing, you are through." As you learn to recognize how you are growing and changing from day to day, you sometimes will be surprised and at other times you will be pleased at the changes you see in yourself.

As your self-awareness grows, you also develop your ability to objectively analyze information, people, and situations. You will be able to see the world from other people's perspectives, discovering how they feel and anticipating what they are likely to think and do. An objective world view helps you to write effectively because you see the world from the perspective of your readers. You will know how to communicate your message in a way your readers will understand it best.

▲ Good Writing: A Creative Process

Writing is not a linear process that goes from point A to point B to point C. It is a creative process that has logical overtones. The process is creative because you are creating something out of nothing. This chapter approaches writing as a process rather than a technical exercise. Although writing has many important technical aspects, the chapter stresses the principles of good written communication. Once you learn these principles, you can apply them to any situation in your life. Mastering this creative process will also help you understand the technical aspects of effective writing.

The communication process can be separated into three steps: planning, translating, and revising.

Plan

- Decide what you want to write about.
- Determine how you will organize your thoughts.
- Establish your writing goal.
- Gather information that will help you achieve your writing goal.
- Sort and organize information.

Translate

- Decide how you will approach your audience.
- Determine what effect you want to have on the reader. Do you want to inform, persuade, or entertain?
- Translate your information into sentences that convey your thoughts and ideas.
- Develop your first draft.

Revise

- Revise your writing until it presents a clear and convincing case to the reader.
- Transform your first draft into a finished product.

This is the basic writing process, accomplished step by step in sequence. The success of each step depends to a great extent on how well you completed the previous steps.

The Four Elements of Effective Writing

One question many students ask is: How can I know if what I have written is any good before I hand in my paper? Lynn Bloom, a well-known writing professor, has identified four elements of effective writing that apply in nearly all situations: content, structure, style, and mechanics.

These elements are very similar to the elements of critical thinking in Benjamin Bloom's taxonomy, because a strong link exists between critical thinking and good writing. You must think clearly to write clearly. You will know that your paper is well written if you pass an objective self-evaluation of your work using the following criteria:

Content

- ❏ Do I have high-quality ideas?
- ❏ Do I have enough ideas?
- ❏ Are my ideas clear?
- ❏ Are my ideas relevant to the central thesis?
- ❏ Do I have logical, basic assumptions and good definitions?
- ❏ Have I completely developed the central thesis?
- ❏ Are my arguments persuasive?
- ❏ Am I open to new perspectives?
- ❏ Do I have reliable outside sources?

Structure

- ❑ What is my focus?
- ❑ How did I organize the material?
- ❑ Do I have good transitions between the parts of the paper?
- ❑ Does my central thesis progress and develop logically?
- ❑ Is my introduction appropriate to the thesis?
- ❑ Is my conclusion appropriate, and does it answer the thesis?

Style

- ❑ Do I choose and arrange my words appropriately?
- ❑ How is my tone? Color? Interest? Originality? Economy of words?

Mechanics

- ❑ Is the punctuation correct?
- ❑ Do I use grammar correctly?
- ❑ Are my sentence structures correct?
- ❑ Are all words spelled correctly?

Lynn Bloom believes that one reason we write is to demonstrate to others that we know the elements of good writing. Educated readers look for these elements so they can grasp more quickly what you have written.

▲ Getting Started

One of the most difficult moments in preparing a paper is getting started. You may ask yourself: What am I going to write about? At this point, it really does not matter. What does matter is that you get started right away. Do not spend a great deal of time worrying about what you should do. If the assignment is a research paper assigned the first week of class and due at the end of the semester, get started right away. Here are some ways to get started.

Establish a project time line with deadlines. First, place these deadlines on your semester-at-a-glance calendar in your official study area (see Chapter 3's discussion of time management skills). A good rule of thumb is to expect to spend 50 percent of your total time on revising your paper after you have written the first rough draft. Be sure to set the completion date at least a week before the paper is due. This will give you more flexibility if things take longer than you expect or if something unforeseen, such as illness, arises. You may also find that the topic is more difficult to research or more complicated to write about than you realized when you started. Regardless of the reason, allow yourself plenty of time to get things done. There is no penalty for finishing early, but severe penalties may result for handing it in late.

Review the assignment carefully. Be sure you know exactly what is expected in your paper. Talk with your professor about the assignment right away. If the assignment is not clear, ask questions: How long should the paper be? What is the objective of the project? Are there examples of previous successful papers that I can look at? May I show you my work as I develop it? Asking questions improves the chances that you will produce the exact type of project your professor expects. There is no need to develop a 50-page paper with 100 references when all you are required to do is a 3-page summary. On the other hand, you would not want to turn in a 3-page paper when your instructor expects 50 pages.

Begin your search for information. The Internet is an excellent place to start your research, but do not overlook libraries. Reference librarians can help you discover many obscure sources of information. They can greatly reduce your research time and increase your sources.

Organize your information. Even in this age of computers, do not forget the power of 3" × 5" cards to help you record and organize your information. Put the information on the front of the card and the source on the back. Immerse yourself in your selected topic. Let your information sources take you where you need to go.

On the Internet, you may find links that will open the doors to many new sources of information. Follow those links, but always check the date and the source. You will want your information to be up to date and come from reputable sources. Not everything you encounter on the Internet or in books is reliable. When in doubt about a source, ask your professor or the reference librarian.

Do not wander too far away from your original topic when you search. For example, if you are doing a geoscience paper on earthquakes and your search takes you to recent movies about earthquakes and the personal lives of the stars of those films, you may have drifted too far away from the original subject.

You may ask: When do I have enough information? The best answer is that you will know when you have enough. Remember, writing is a creative process. If your assignment is to write a 50-page paper that counts as 80 percent of your semester grade, you will want to gather much more information and do much more work than for a 3-page paper worth 5 percent of your grade.

Once your information search is complete, take a few moments to reflect on what you have learned about your topic. More than likely, you will have gained considerable insight into the subject through your research. For example, if your paper is about how a change in government policy affected the economy of Peru, you may now realize that the issue is much more complex. You may have discovered that some of these changes in the economy resulted from shifts in the balance of trade and changes in the currency exchange rates. Because of this new information, you may choose to shift the focus of your paper to include the role of trade balances and currency exchange rates. Broadening your subject to include these two new areas may allow you to explain more fully the changes in the general economy of Peru. The result is a deeper understanding of the situation and the potential for a higher grade on the paper.

You can also objectively analyze your information at this point, and may realize that your original assessment of events in Peru is incomplete. As an active learner, you actually are critically evaluating your research information. You have allowed the new information uncovered during your information search to lead you to a broader objective for your paper. Next, you will need to find supporting arguments for this broader position. You may want to arrange your 3" x 5" cards in a way that builds a logical argument. You can make this transition because your mind is actively engaged in understanding how your data have guided you to a revised objective.

CRITICAL THINKING

Exercise 7.1 *Bring to class two or three news magazines or journals. Read and evaluate three articles by answering the questions in the source assessment in Figure 7.1 (one assessment for each article). At the end of each assessment, explain why you would or would not use this source for a college paper.*

▲ Developing Your First Draft

Many people tend to think: Writing comes easily and words just pour out—for everyone but me. That statement could not be further from the truth. Good writing requires time, hard work, and revisions, but it is available to just about anyone. Many well-known authors tell about struggling for words or writing and rewriting a famous passage 20 or 30 times before getting the words just

FIGURE 7.1 **Source Assessment**

Name of magazine: _____

Title of article: _____

Author of article: _____

Date of article: _____

Why should you believe this author? _____

_____

What are the author's credentials? _____

_____

Who published the article? _____

Did the article originally come from another source (a book, another maga-

zine)? If so, what is that source? _____

Explain why you would or would not use this article in your writing plan.

_____

_____

right. A classic written work rarely happens the first time a writer puts down an idea on paper. Getting your rough ideas down on paper is what your first draft is all about.

When you have collected all the information you need, arrange it in a logical sequence. First, lay out your 3" x 5" cards in a logical order on a table or on the floor. Then develop a formal written outline from this sequence. Since each card contains just one fact or quote, you can move the cards around until you have a plan that makes sense to you. Once you have a plan, decide how you will express your thoughts clearly to others. You are now ready to develop the first draft of your paper.

Your goal should be to keep the words and ideas flowing. First, construct a thesis statement based on your research. Decide whether you intend to describe something or persuade the reader. Then start writing, using the outline you developed earlier as a rough guide. Do not stop until you have it all down on paper. Be sure to backtrack and make changes as you find better ways to explain things. Do not worry yet how it looks or sounds; the first draft is only for you. After you finish your first draft, let it rest, at least overnight.

Often a paper that sounded so good when you wrote it loses its luster when you reread it a day or two later. Do not be discouraged by this. In one part of your paper, you may be surprised by your keen insight and eloquent use of the English language; in another part, you may be horrified by what you wrote. This is a normal part of the paper development process. Again, your first priority is to get your ideas down on paper.

After letting your first draft rest for a while, you should evaluate it to determine if you have covered all the relevant points. Did you leave out any important information? Is your approach appropriate for your audience? Does your organization accomplish your writing objective? If the answer to any of these questions is *no*, you will need to backtrack and fix the things that are wrong. Sometimes the "holes" in your information or logic are not apparent until you write them down. You will need sufficient time to develop your project in your mind and on the paper. When you have completed your revisions, write a second draft and evaluate it to see if you get *yes* answers to the preceding questions. When all answers are *yes*, you are on your way to writing a paper that meets your expectations. Now it is time to develop a final paper that will communicate your ideas effectively to your intended audience.

In the following exercises, you will be building the structure of a research paper. Although you will not be writing a complete paper, you will simulate the process with a small amount of research.

CRITICAL THINKING

Exercise 7.2 *Write a thesis statement that relates to an important topic in your major. Be sure it presents a specific problem that will be answered in your paper.*

_____

_____

_____

_____

CRITICAL THINKING

Exercise 7.3 *Write a thesis statement that relates to a topic in your major. Your statement should attempt to persuade your audience about a specific issue.*

_____

_____

_____

_____

Exercise 7.4 *Using your thesis statement in Exercise 7.3, write down three supporting arguments. (Remember, this is a planning exercise. You are writing this without the benefit of a lot of research, so your arguments may not be totally accurate.)*

_____

_____

_____

Exercise 7.5 *Draft an introduction for your paper. Be sure it clearly presents your thesis statement from Exercise 7.3. (Remember, this is a planning exercise.)*

Exercise 7.6 *Draft a conclusion for your paper. Be sure you come to a complete, persuasive conclusion to the thesis statement you chose in Exercise 7.3.*

Exercise 7.7 *Structure the body of your paper. Focus on making the content significant with evidence of supporting claims and clear details. Include some complex issues and arguments, as well as analytical and descriptive passages. (Remember, you are not writing a complete paper; you are devising a plan for a research paper.)*

▲ The Finished Product

TRANSFORMING PROSE INTO RHETORIC

Now you are well on your way to a successful paper. You have clearly identified the thesis and logically laid out the arguments you need to support it. But remember that if you want to communicate successfully, your audience must understand what you are saying. It is not enough to develop information that makes sense only to you. Since you are writing a college paper, you will need to communicate well with your professor or whomever else will be grading your project. Someday your audience may be a supervisor or an important client. Then you will have much more than a grade at stake. In either case, clear writing is important to effective communication.

At some point, you must transform your writing from prose to rhetoric. This is when you move from being merely a technically correct writer to becoming a skilled artist who can accomplish things with words. You will also be a writer who can uplift, inspire, entertain, or persuade others through the power of words.

Years ago, college students took courses in rhetoric. These classes were designed to teach students how to use language effectively, persuasively, and eloquently. The goal was for students to elevate their writing skills above the simple prose used in everyday conversation. Though today the name of this course may vary among colleges, rhetoric, or the effective use of language, is still the objective of college writing courses.

Rhetoric is what gives more power to your ideas and words. It is the difference between "four score and seven years ago" and "87 years ago." It is what makes "to be or not to be" more powerful than "maybe I will, or maybe I won't." The words convey the same meaning, but their impact differs sharply. By elevating your words from prose to rhetoric, you will enhance the effectiveness of your work. If you apply a few simple principles to your prose, you will raise your writing to rhetoric:

1. *Recognize that the polishing process takes time.* Anticipate that you will devote 50 percent of your preparation time to revising.

2. *Take a one- or two-day cooling-off period between the development of the first draft and the start of your revisions.* This will give you time to think about what you actually wrote and restore your objectivity. It will also give you time to rebuild your creative reserves.

3. *Read your rough draft aloud.* This lets you see and hear any errors in your writing. If words or phrases do not sound right, you need to edit them. Then read your draft aloud again, continuing to make changes until you hear a presentation that flows well and is constructed logically. Determine if your writing is appropriate for your intended audience and whether it meets your intended purpose. When you can read your paper aloud with very few changes, you have successfully completed this stage of the process.

4. *Check the spelling and grammar.* Use a good word processing program that has spelling and grammar checks. Then check carefully for errors the program may not catch. For instance, a computer program will not distinguish between *threw* and *through* or among *to, too,* and *two.*

5. *Let someone else proofread your revised paper.* An outside perspective and a different pair of eyes can give you an objective opinion on how well you met your goals and how effectively you used language. This type of feedback can be tough on the ego, but if done constructively it will greatly enhance the quality of your work. Evaluate the proofreader's comments and incorporate them into the next revision of your paper.

Few things take as much work as a good research paper. Your paper will bring you great intellectual satisfaction if you are willing to invest the time, attention, and energy needed to make it happen. Like the marathon runner preparing for the race, you will get stronger and more proficient each time you write.

Exercise 7.8 *Bring to class your most recent research paper or writing assignment. Team up with a classmate and read each other's writing, asking questions for clarification. Evaluate the content, and identify the strengths of your partner's paper. Then write three recommendations for improvement. Be specific.*

_____

_____

_____

_____

_____

Exercise 7.9 *Bring to class a paper you have recently written. Pair up with another student and exchange papers. Proofread each other's papers, looking for good rhetoric, proper sentence structure, and correct grammar. Discuss what you have found with your partner. Write a paragraph about the main things you learned from your peer reviewer.*

Exercise 7.10 *As a critical thinker/writer, you probably incorporate into your writing several levels of Bloom's taxonomy. Bring in one of your recent writing assignments and identify the specific levels of Bloom's cognitive and affective domains in the paper. What levels of Bloom's taxonomy are not found in your writing? Write a paragraph explaining why your paper does not include the other levels.*

Exercise 7.11 *In the library or on the Internet, find an article from a technical journal. Then find an article from a news magazine such as* Time *or* Newsweek. *Bring these articles to class and discuss in a small group how and why these two articles are different. Write one paragraph to communicate your group's findings and conclusions.*

Exercise 7.12 *Assume one of your classmates wrote a paper in which he used language that demeans women. The rest of the class finds the language offensive, but the writer feels strongly that it is essential to expressing his idea. If you were the professor, how would you respond to this paper? Would you lower the grade because of the language? Explain why or why not. What would you do if the language broke any laws? On a separate piece of paper, write a paragraph communicating your response to this student's controversial paper.*

Exercise 7.13 *Compare thinking and writing. On a separate piece of paper, describe in a paragraph how they relate to each other.*

Exercise 7.14 *Write a letter to a family member or a close friend describing your first few weeks of college. Be creative, and be sure to communicate your ideas so the reader will understand what you mean.*

Exercise 7.15 *In a small group, discuss each person's writing strengths. Report to the entire class what major areas of strength you identified in your group. Return to your group and discuss each person's writing weaknesses. Report to the entire class what major areas of weakness you identified in your group. Again return to your group and write down some strategies that will strengthen each person's writing skills. Share with the entire class at least three writing strategies your group's members will employ to improve their writing skills.*

_____

_____

_____

_____

Exercise 7.16 *Each student is asked to identify and describe ten areas in which writing is or will be an important part of his or her life. In class, in "round robin" style, each student presents an area that she or he identified. One student writes down each area on the board as it is shared. Students continue taking turns identifying their areas until all students have exhausted their lists. Then the class votes for the top three areas in which writing is important. (Number them from 1 to 3 on the board, with number 1 being the most important.) Did the consensus surprise you? Why do you think these three areas made it to the top? Did any of your areas make the top three? Why or why not?*

Exercise 7.17 *Analyze what students mean when they say that they "cannot write." Identify the typical reasons given for being unable to write well. Write a plan for these students (it may include you) that will help them gain more confidence in their writing abilities.*

CHAPTER HIGHLIGHTS

1. A good education means you can think critically rather than just remember facts.

2. One way you show that you can think well is to write clearly.

3. Writing well is important throughout your life.

4. Preparing a paper will help you clarify what you are thinking.

5. Explaining something to someone else is a good way to test your knowledge.

6. Developing your sense of self-awareness is a good way to see the world from another person's perspective. Understanding many perspectives allows you to speak or write in a way your audience will understand clearly.

7. Preparing a paper is a creative process since it makes something out of nothing.

8. Good writing requires that you know what you want to communicate and that you devote enough time and hard work to fully developing your ideas.

9. Your research data should lead you to the objective of your written presentation.

10. Always evaluate the reliability of your information sources.

11. The first draft is only for you, the author, to see. The objective is to get all your ideas in writing and arrange them in some logical order.

12. Your finished product should elevate your writing from prose to rhetoric so your words have more power.

13. Read your draft aloud to yourself to discover any errors in your writing. Then have a peer proofread and critique your draft.

14. Practice will make you a better writer.

CHAPTER HIGHLIGHTS

CASE STUDY

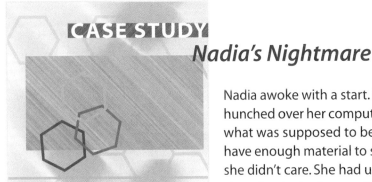

Nadia's Nightmare

Nadia awoke with a start. For the second time tonight, she had fallen asleep hunched over her computer. It was 3:45 A.M., and she was still on page four of what was supposed to be a ten-page paper. Nadia was not sure she would have enough material to stretch what she had to ten pages, but at this hour she didn't care. She had until 9:00 A.M. to get this paper done for her writing class. As she had many times before, she had promised herself she would start writing when the assignment was given out, but she always hit a road-block because she just did not consider herself a writer. Nadia knew she would be so worn out from writing that she would sneak into class, drop off the paper in the pile, and go get some sleep. Since her 10:00 A.M. math class was just to get back a test and go over it, she figured she could skip that class and pick up her test later. If she got some sleep, she should be coherent for her biology lab that afternoon.

This was Nadia's third paper of the semester, and she still had five more to go. This paper was the worst one so far. She had to summarize the essence of Ralph Waldo Emerson's collection of essays titled *Self-Reliance* and describe how they are useful today. Thank goodness a senior literature major down the hall had summarized the book for her, since all she had time to do was skim it. Her professor, Dr. Alter, seemed to make a bigger deal out of this book than all the others the class had read so far. She required at least ten pages for this paper rather than the normal three-page summary for all the others. It was hard to make much sense of all the things Emerson talked about. What did prudence, self-reliance, and intellect have to do with an 18-year-old college freshman? Dr. Alter saw things in the essays that Nadia would never have seen in a hundred years. The material Nadia found on the Internet about the life of Emerson did help her fill up one page of the paper, but she never felt confident that she understood what transcendentalism is all about. She reread her notes in her spiral-bound notebook, but had a hard time making any sense out of them. Nadia also had a hard time under-standing why, as a biology major, she had to take these silly courses anyway.

It had only been a week since the class had discussed Emerson's essays. That was the last time Nadia had looked at her notes. Although she remem-bered little about the discussion, she just kept pounding her computer key-board, hoping something good would appear on the page. This approach had always worked for her in high school, but, given her low grades on the first two papers, she was not sure it would help her out in this course.

Describe Nadia's approach to this writing assignment. What changes, if any, would you make in her approach? How would you respond to her comment that these "silly courses" were a waste of time for a biology major?

Personal Journal

CRITICAL THINKING

Personal Journal 7.1 Describe a writing assignment that went well. What factors helped you to do well? Describe a writing assignment that went poorly. What factors caused you to do poorly? What are your biggest roadblocks to being a consistently good writer? What are you doing to overcome them?

_____

_____

_____

_____

_____

_____

_____

DIVERSITY

Personal Journal 7.2 Many people believe that good writing comes from one's own experiences. If that is true, the best preparation for becoming a good writer is to experience and appreciate as many different cultures, traditions, and situations as you can. Do you agree or disagree with this statement? Explain your answer. Give one example where experience is a prerequisite for good writing.

_____

_____

_____

_____

_____

_____

_____

CHAPTER QUIZ

1. Explain why good writing is important to a good education.

   _____

   _____

   _____

   _____

2. Describe the roles of a keen sense of self-awareness and active learning in good writing.

   _____

   _____

   _____

   _____

3. Explain why and how good writing is a process.

   _____

   _____

   _____

   _____

4. Discuss how clear thinking, time management, and hard work are important to good writing.

   _____

   _____

   _____

   _____

ADDITIONAL RESOURCES

Noonan, Peggy. *On Speaking Well.* New York: Regan Books, 1998.

Strunk, W., & E. B. White. *The Elements of Style.* 4th ed. Needham Heights, MA: Allyn & Bacon, 2000.

CHAPTER 8

Research Skills

After reading this chapter, you will understand why:

- Computerized library information systems and the Internet have changed the way you do research for a term paper.
- Computerized library information systems and the Internet have changed the balance of power of information.
- It takes an active learner to properly manage information.

After reading this chapter, you will know how to:

- Carry out an information search in the library.
- Conduct an information search on the Internet.
- Utilize a reference librarian in researching a paper.

Today having good research skills is much more than just knowing your way around the library. Research resources have expanded to allow you access to a huge world of information both in and out of your local library. Never before in the history of civilization have so many people been given such quick, easy access to so much information. With a few computer keystrokes, you can have the latest information on just about any topic from anywhere on the globe. However, it is easy to become overwhelmed by all the information available. Knowing how to evaluate and effectively use all this information is part of being a wise, active learner.

For many years, professors have used research papers and projects as a way for students to learn how to find, organize, and report on information. The research process is a great deal easier today. No longer do you need to spend hours in the dark corners of a library searching for a book. Today you can do your work better, more thoroughly, and more quickly from a computer at your home, dorm room, study space, or library.

When the number of people with personal computers and access to the Internet dramatically increased in the 1990s, the world changed the way it operates. Countless people with basic computer skills, a personal computer, a modem, and

a telephone line developed web sites that instantly made their information available to the world. Some Internet entrepreneurs made fortunes by offering their ideas online. The "information highway" gave people greater control of data and the power to learn more at a faster rate. It also diminished the role of those who previously controlled information. The speed of change became more rapid, and new information became available and was disseminated faster than ever before.

Today it is impossible to keep up with all the web sites and information systems available on the Internet. They are changing so rapidly that by the time you read this book, the information will have changed. For this reason, this chapter focuses on the process of information management rather than on how to navigate the numerous information sources. You will learn about the principles of information management that have endured through years of rapid change.

▲ Getting Started

The most difficult part of any project is getting started. If your professor requires you to gather information beyond what is available in your notes and readings, you may well wonder where to begin. First, you prepare yourself by taking a student success course such as this one. Then you learn about your library: where it is, where items are located, what information services are available, and who can help you find information. A library tour will be helpful, either a self-guided tour or a personalized tour with a reference librarian. Reference librarians are the "guardian angels" of the information age who keep you on the right path in your search for the best information. They can suggest the right keywords for your information search, tell you about the latest information sources, or locate a hard-to-find book.

HOW THE LIBRARY IS ORGANIZED

The library remains the major access point for all types of information. Library resources should be a vital part of your information search.

Libraries typically have three major sections: stacks, references, and periodicals.

- The **stacks** house most of the books. Open stacks are available to anyone, whereas access to closed stacks is limited to library personnel.

- The **reference section** has items that cannot be checked out so they are available at all times. They are usually high-demand items such as encyclopedias, handbooks, industry and trade association publications, yearly summaries of statistics, and so on.

- The **periodical section** contains publications that are published daily, weekly, monthly, quarterly, or annually, such as newspapers, magazines, academic journals, and annual business reports.

In addition to these three sections, many libraries have sections devoted to maps, U.S. government documents, local history, and audio or video equipment.

Most libraries now have a computer section where Internet access is available. Librarians can help you access the Internet and use its powerful search engines. Nearly all libraries have their inventory of available materials online. These systems are easy to use and tell you what the library has, where the material can be found, and whether it is currently available. Many library information systems have access to other libraries all over the world.

USING ENCYCLOPEDIAS

When researching a topic about which you know very little, an encyclopedia is a great place to start. An encyclopedia provides concise information about a topic so you can get an overall picture of the major ideas and concepts. Encyclopedias can be very helpful when researching historical information, but the material on rapidly moving fields such as the sciences and technology may be dated.

Most encyclopedia articles end with a list of other references that you can use to continue your information search. In addition to general encyclopedias, there are many specific subject encyclopedias that will provide greater detail on more specific topics. A reference librarian can help you find these items. If you prefer working on a computer, many general encyclopedias are now on CD-ROM or can be accessed online. This makes it easy for you to incorporate encyclopedias into your initial information search.

CONDUCTING A LIBRARY INFORMATION SEARCH

Most online library information systems are set up so you can search for information by title, by author, or by keyword.

- In a **title search**, you type in the exact title of a book or publication. This is the most direct search route.

- In an **author search**, you type in an author's name to see all the publications by that author that are in the library system. This type of search is best when you know the author's name but do not have the full title of the book.

- A **keyword search** tends to be much broader and sometimes more complicated. First, you must use a properly defined keyword in your search. For example, if you type the word *hunger*, you may find that the library has more than 1,000 items with that word in the title. If you refine your keyword search to *hunger + United States + rural Pennsylvania*, you may get a more manageable list of ten titles. Then all you need to do is print out the list and go find the available publications. In a short period of time, you will have conducted a powerful, exhaustive search of the entire library that in the past might have taken several days.

    What should you do if you find no useful information about your topic using the keyword *hunger*? This is where your reference librarian can help. Although this person will not do the search for you, he or she will advise you on how to adjust your search procedures to yield better results. For instance, if you used *food* as the keyword in your information search, you would get a very different list of publications.

▲ *Information and the Internet*

The Internet has expanded the breadth and depth of information available to the world. You no longer have to visit the library to gain access to all the best information. Anything on the Web is available to everyone with Internet access, no matter where one is. The ability to use this system is critical to every student's success and therefore should be a part of every student success course. Most schools have computer labs so every student has access to a personal computer and associated software for word processing, spreadsheets, graphics, and the Internet.

Computer literacy is quickly becoming a required skill in a person's education and career. Most schools now equip dormitory rooms with computer hookups so students can connect their personal computers to the campus network. Other schools provide a dial-up network from any telephone. Some schools provide wireless access where students can turn on their computers and have Internet access anywhere on campus. Many students also enjoy the benefits of email, which allows them to send messages instantaneously, with a single keystroke, to friends and family around the world.

Just as you must evaluate the credibility of published material in the library, you must assess the information on the Internet, but even more closely. You should assess the quality, reliability, and sources of all Internet articles. If you have any doubts about the quality of your Internet information, you may need to do some research on the source to find out if it is a reliable author or organization. Also, remember to talk with your reference librarian or your professor about material you have found.

Exercise 8.1 *In a group of three or four students, formulate a question related to one of your current courses. Identify the sources of information you might use to answer this question—journals, books, periodicals, web sites, etc. (You will need to do some library and Internet searching to come up with a good list of sources.) Then identify the level of Bloom's affective and cognitive domains that each of these sources reflects.*

_____

_____

_____

_____

_____

Exercise 8.2 *Examine five Internet sources that relate to one of your courses. On a separate sheet of paper, cite each source and briefly describe what information it provides for the course.*

Exercise 8.3 *Research the most current copyright laws. What do they say about copying? About plagiarism? What parts of the law are most relevant to you as a student?*

_____

_____

_____

_____

_____

ETHICS

Exercise 8.4 *You and a close friend are taking the same course. Instead of doing the same research for papers together, you take turns, then share the results of your research with each other. Do you think this practice is acceptable, or is it a form of cheating? Explain your answer.*

_____

_____

_____

_____

ETHICS

Exercise 8.5 *You and a close friend are taking the same course. Instead of buying two copies of the same book, you both chip in for one book and, since it is short, go to the copy machine and make a second copy for a fraction of the cost. Discuss in class whether this practice is good economical planning or breaking the law.*

ACTIVE LEARNING

Exercise 8.6 *Visit your college library and introduce yourself to the reference librarian who oversees the collections related to your major. What is this person's name? Describe in a few sentences how this person will be most helpful to you.*

_____

_____

_____

_____

Exercise 8.7 *On a separate sheet of paper, list at least three differences between your high school library and your college library. Explain these differences in a short essay. Describe one way your college library will help you become a better active learner.*

Exercise 8.8 *Choose a broad topic in an area that interests you. Write down six keywords that relate to your topic. Conduct a computerized library search of each keyword and write down the number of publications that come up for each. Now refine your search by writing down six more specific keywords. Write down the number of publications that come up for this search. Make a list of at least two publications for each of your keywords that most closely match your topic. Explain in a paragraph how you conducted this search and how you could narrow down the number of citations.*

Exercise 8.9 *Choose a broad topic in an area that interests you. Write down six keywords that relate to your topic. Conduct an Internet search for each keyword and write down the number of web links you find for each. Now refine your search by entering six more specific keywords. Write down the number of web links that come up for this search. Make a list of at least two web sites for each of your keywords that most closely match your topic. Explain in a paragraph how you conducted this search and how you could narrow down the number of web sites.*

Exercise 8.10 *On a separate sheet of paper, develop an evaluation sheet to assess the reliability of six web sites that you found in your search in Exercise 8.9. If a specific author is indicated, evaluate the credibility of that author.*

Exercise 8.11 *You discover an Internet document that has no identified author. Describe how you might prove the document's credibility and legitimately incorporate the information into a research paper.*

Exercise 8.12 *Compare the major differences between a technical journal and a popular magazine. Choose an article from each type of publication and compare the two articles in the following areas: type of publication, credibility of the author, information found in the narrative, recency of the information, intent of the publication, and the intended audience.*

CHAPTER HIGHLIGHTS

1. Good research skills include the ability to handle information both in and out of the library.

2. To be a successful manager of information, you must be an active learner.

3. The combination of the Internet and online library information systems has put more information at one's fingertips than ever before possible.

4. Open access to information has changed the power structure of the world.

5. Ready access to information means people can make better decisions and have greater control over their lives.

6. Research papers and projects teach you how to find, organize, and report information. This process is accomplished more effectively through the use of computers and library information systems.

7. A library typically has three major sections: stacks, references, and periodicals.

8. The library should be the center of your information search since it specializes in information management. The reference librarian is a vital resource that can help you in your search.

9. Encyclopedias are a good place to begin your information search.

10. Library information systems and the Internet place everyone at the center of the information world. Be sure to evaluate the information you discover, since not all of it will be of equal quality.

CHAPTER HIGHLIGHTS

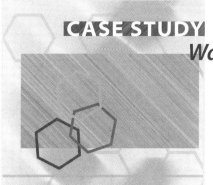

CASE STUDY
Wandering Wanda

It was 10:45 P.M., the normal closing time for the reference desk at the library. The reference librarian was closing things up for the evening when a very frustrated young student appeared. Wanda introduced herself and asked the librarian if she remembered meeting her several weeks ago when her student success class toured the library and learned about its information system. The librarian politely responded that she did not remember Wanda but asked if she could help her.

"I've been wandering around in the stacks since 7:00 P.M. and I can't find anything I'm looking for. Can you help me?" Wanda asked. The librarian told Wanda that she should have stopped by the reference desk sooner since she had been on duty since 4:00 P.M. Wanda said she had been confident that she could find everything she needed on her own. "It all seemed so easy when you explained it to the class during the tour. Besides, you looked very busy, and I didn't want to bother you just for some freshman's research paper," said Wanda.

Once Wanda calmed down, she told the librarian all about her assignment. Unfortunately, Wanda had lost the sheet describing her research paper that her entomology professor had given out because she had stuffed it into her spiral-bound notebook. She was sure she remembered most of the details. The paper had to have at least five references, with no more than two of them coming from the Internet. It had to be between 15 and 20 pages long and double-spaced using a standard-size type. Wanda said she felt really lost on this assignment since she was a first-year American literature major writing on the economic impact of biotechnology on the need for honeybees in plant pollination. She explained that she had taken this course only to meet a university graduation requirement in the sciences and had been assigned the topic by her professor.

Once the librarian heard of Wanda's plight and found out that the paper was not due until next week, she asked her to come back the next day when there would be more time. She gave Wanda a list of things to do between now and then.

What do you think the librarian asked Wanda to do before they met again? What mistakes did Wanda make in her approach to this paper? What did she do right?

Personal Journal

SELF-AWARENESS

Personal Journal 8.1 How has this chapter changed your view of the library? What value do you think the library has in your education? Describe three ways you will use the library or reference librarians when you prepare your next research paper or project.

_____

_____

_____

_____

_____

_____

_____

_____

SELF-AWARENESS

Personal Journal 8.2 How has this chapter changed your view of the Internet? What value do you think the Internet has in your education? Describe three ways you will use the Internet when you prepare your next research paper or project.

_____

_____

_____

_____

_____

_____

_____

_____

CHAPTER QUIZ

1. How do the Internet and library information systems change the balance of the power of knowledge?

   _____

   _____

   _____

   _____

   _____

2. Outline the steps you should follow in conducting a keyword search on a topic.

   _____

   _____

   _____

   _____

   _____

3. When is the Internet the best source of information? When is it not a good source? Explain your answer.

   _____

   _____

   _____

   _____

   _____

CHAPTER 9

Critical Thinking Skills

CHAPTER OBJECTIVES

After reading this chapter, you will understand why:

- You must have the right attitude toward learning, as well as the right skills.
- Your ability to identify the components of critical thinking is essential in all your subjects.
- You need to evaluate the elements of critical thinking arguments.
- You become a more successful student when you apply critical thinking.
- People learn differently.
- It is important for you to know your learning style.
- Mind mapping can enhance your learning.

After reading this chapter, you will know how to:

- Think critically.
- Differentiate between facts and opinions.
- Recognize your learning style.
- Develop and apply mind mapping.

FRONT VIEW

A primary goal of this course is to transform you into a critical thinker. Critical thinking is a prerequisite to success because it gives you the problem-solving skills needed to meet the challenges of college and lifelong learning. Although good skills and techniques are necessary ingredients of success, they do not ensure it. You must have the critical thinking skills that endure time and adapt to different circumstances.

▲ The Role of Attitude in Critical Thinking

The attitudes necessary to be a good critical thinker were described by the famous philosopher John Dewey in his 1933 classic book, *How We Think*. Dewey believed that attitude is a key ingredient in how well we think:

> What can be done, however, is to cultivate those attitudes that are favorable to the use of the best methods of inquiry and testing. Knowledge of the methods alone will not suffice; there must be the desire, the will, to employ them. This desire is an affair of personal disposition. But on the other hand, the disposition alone will not suffice. There must also be understanding of the forms and techniques that are the channels through which these attitudes operate to best advantage.

Dewey defined those attitudes as *open-mindedness, wholeheartedness,* and *responsibility*.

A student who is **open-minded** is free of bias and willing to accept new ideas. This student will listen to a variety of perspectives and give each one full attention. Bear in mind that open-mindedness is not "empty-mindedness." Dewey said,

> [Open-mindedness] includes an active desire to listen to more sides than one; to give heed to facts from whatever source they come; to give full attention to alternative possibilities; to recognize the possibility of error even in the beliefs that are dearest to us. . . . [Mental sluggishness] can best be fought by cultivating that alert curiosity and spontaneous outreaching for the new which is the essence of the open mind. The mind that is open merely in the sense that it passively permits things to trickle in and through will not be able to resist the factors that make for mental closure.

An attitude of open-mindedness is important if you want to become an *active learner.*

Wholeheartedness is related to a student's passion for inquiry. Dewey regards genuine enthusiasm as an attitude that fosters intellectual growth:

> When a person is absorbed, the subject carries him on. Questions occur to him spontaneously; a flood of suggestions pour in on him; further inquiries and readings are indicated and followed; instead of having to use his energy to hold his mind to the subject, the material holds and buoys his mind up and gives an onward impetus to thinking. A genuine enthusiasm is an attitude that operates as an intellectual force.

Wholeheartedness is important if you want to make a *personal commitment* to success in college and in life.

Responsibility is a moral attitude that accepts the logical consequences of a particular belief. As Dewey put it,

> To be intellectually responsible is to consider the consequences of a projected step; it means to be willing to adopt these consequences when they follow reasonably from any position already taken. Intellectual responsibility secures integrity; that is to say, consistency and harmony in belief.

This attitude is important if you want to take *personal responsibility* for the things that happen in your life.

By whatever name you call them, these three attitudes are prerequisites for success. Each makes it easier for you to accomplish your goals. By being an open-minded, wholehearted, responsible learner, you will more easily rise to the highest levels of Bloom's taxonomy of the cognitive domain and become a critical thinker.

Open-minded **+** Whole-hearted **+** Responsible **=** **CRITICAL THINKING**

HOW ATTITUDE AFFECTS CRITICAL THINKING

A good way to explain critical thinking is with an example. Joe, a college freshman, was in a history class in which his professor told the class that George Washington was one of the world's greatest dictators. The statement struck Joe immediately as an outrageous untruth, and he felt the teacher had to be an unpatriotic Benedict Arnold. So Joe quit listening and started to think how he might drop the course. Joe never asked himself or his professor why he would describe Washington as a dictator and assumed the professor did not know what he was talking about.

What Joe should have done was evaluate the statement and question its accuracy. The professor's goal may have been to get the students to think about the statement and to question it. Many students believe that whatever a professor says must be true—that all information given in class is black and white, with no gray areas. From Joe's perspective, the professor was incompetent. Other students in the class were puzzled by the statement, and still others wondered what the term *dictator* meant. In the end, all the students either accepted, rejected, or ignored the statement.

A critical thinker would do the following in a similar situation:

1. Think actively. A wholehearted student would listen to and evaluate what is being said to understand the context of the statement. This helps students to properly assess what the professor is really trying to say. Sometimes a professor makes a controversial statement to see if students are paying attention. Other times, a professor aims to spark students to think and participate in a class discussion.

2. Think of examples that prove the statement.

3. Think of examples that disprove the statement.

4. Think of specific things that support the different perspectives.

5. Seek the views of others on this topic.

6. Draw your own conclusions with appropriate supporting facts and arguments.

THE ROLE OF QUESTIONING

Questions are important to strengthening your ability as a critical thinker. Asking questions is a natural part of growing up and something we all did as children. Most parents remember all the times their toddler asked, "What's this?" When this happened over and over again, they knew their child was thinking and learning. As children grow and mature, they acquire better thinking and language skills that allow them to understand more and formulate more complex questions. The questions you ask now are what transform you into a critical thinker.

By asking questions, you request more information to help you clarify, expand, or justify your understanding. When you ask **clarifying questions**, you attempt to verify the accuracy of the information you received. You might do this by restating the information in your own words. Clarifying questions help you to operate at the lowest levels of the cognitive domain (knowledge and comprehension). **Expanding questions** are the product of your analysis and evaluation of new knowledge you receive. These questions move you to higher levels of the cognitive domain (application, analysis, and synthesis). When you ask **justification questions**, you show your ability to draw conclusions, test the internal consistency of data, and relate what was presented to other facts. At this point, your thinking skills are at their highest levels of the cognitive domain (evaluation). You reveal a great deal about yourself and your critical thinking abilities by the way you formulate your questions.

THE DIFFERENCE BETWEEN FACTS AND OPINIONS

The ability to create language is one attribute that distinguishes humans from the rest of the animal kingdom. A spoken language allows humans to express their thoughts to others at a given moment. A written language enables humans to express their thoughts to others at different times and places. Thanks to language, humans create relationships, build governments, and convey information to one another. As the amount of new information grows every day, their ability to make sense of it all demands more critical thinking skills to distinguish fact from opinion. Separating facts from opinions, especially in religion and politics, explains the sources of conflicts throughout much of human history.

When dealing with new information, it is important to be able to sort between statements of *fact* and statements of *opinion*. This is not always an easy task. You must decide whether or not the ideas presented are supported by reasonable statements of evidence that validate the opinion. Because of the limits of time and money, it is impossible to completely and absolutely test the validity of every argument you encounter. Instead, you can seek evidence that increases the probability that something is true and accurate. In the end, when you must decide the validity of an opinion, all you can do is assess the quality of the supporting evidence.

A critical thinker can use four different steps to arrive at a thoughtful conclusion:

1. Construct questions to independently clarify the questions and problems being dealt with

2. Organize and develop plans to form a logical argument; identify the supporting evidence that relates to the question as well as the opposing evidence

3. Test each piece of evidence on both sides for truthfulness and context

4. Develop a logical argument based on the evidence that will prove or disprove the claim being made

▲ How Your Brain Learns

In the past few years, scientists have uncovered a lot of information about how the brain functions. Knowing how your brain works will help you become a better critical thinker. Educators are using this new knowledge to develop novel strategies for learning and teaching at all levels of education. Big changes are occurring at the college level as professors are increasingly abandoning the lecture format to appeal to a greater variety of student learning styles.

Research on brain function shows that different types of thinking and reasoning occur in different parts of the brain. The left lobe of the brain handles most verbal processing, including information related to logical and analytical operations and the sorting and filing of details. The right lobe handles most visual and spatial processing. This includes emotions, creative activities, and analysis of broad concepts and principles.

On the basis of this knowledge, some people characterize college as a place where those who have strong verbal processing skills do well. These "left-brained" people do well at the tasks traditionally important to success in college: sorting and filing details given in textbook readings and classroom lectures. Those students who prefer to listen to lectures, take notes, and read their notes back to themselves aloud exhibit an auditory learning style. They learn best by listening. Those who prefer professors who write extensively on the blackboard and who enjoy outlining the material in the book exhibit a visual learning style. They learn best by observing things.

The bias of college success toward efficient verbal processors has perpetuated itself because those who possess this learning style are the ones most likely to become professors. However, the latest findings of scientists and educators reveal that learning styles are much more diverse. Instructors have had to reassess their teaching and learning methods, thus causing a revolution in college teaching and intensifying the search to find better ways to teach and learn.

LONG-TERM AND SHORT-TERM MEMORY

The brain can absorb huge amounts of information, but it retains only the things that it considers important. If your brain did not work this way, you would be overwhelmed with information and most likely unable to remember anything. The decision your brain makes about what is important and worthy of remembering is based largely on how often you encounter the piece of data. Items you use only once, such as certain telephone numbers, are quickly forgotten; items that you encounter repeatedly, such as a theme song from a television show you watch every day, are retained.

Our memory is separated into short-term memory and long-term memory. Your goal as a student is to move as much as possible of what is presented in a course into long-term memory. Long-term memory is like a huge, permanent warehouse. Because of its enormous size, the warehouse must be well organized so you can easily find everything stored there. You quickly recall the things you use frequently from your long-term memory, such as your home telephone number, social security number, and zip code. Items used infrequently, such as the name of your third-grade teacher, may take a while to remember, but they are still in the storage warehouse of your memory.

How do you get new information from short-term to long-term memory? Information in the first part of short-term memory is what is on your mind right now. This is where you store a telephone number from the time you see it in the telephone book until you have dialed it. Once you have finished the call, you normally forget the number.

The second part of short-term memory is where you store information for a limited time while the brain decides whether it is worth passing on to long-term

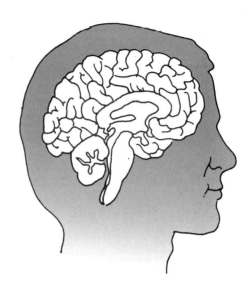

memory. Some characterize this second stage as the "use it or lose it" period. If new information is not reinforced by using it again within a short time, it is not sent to long-term memory, and it is lost. It is estimated that up to half the new information you receive is lost within 24 hours if not used. In Chapter 3, you were encouraged to review your class notes for 20 minutes before and after each class and to study each subject every day for 20 to 30 minutes so the data will go into long-term memory.

The reason "all-nighters" rarely work is that the information you cram into your brain remains in the second part of your short-term memory for only a brief period. Since you typically do not use the crammed information again within 24 hours, it is lost. If the next test on this subject requires any information from this cramming session, it will not be in your long-term memory. You will be forced to go back and learn the material again. The secret of processing information into long-term memory involves frequent reinforcement through many short study and review sessions.

LEARNING AND MEMORIZATION

As you attempt to store things in long-term memory, you need to understand the difference between learning and memorization. You may be accustomed to studying for a test by memorizing facts and then repeating them back. You probably did this when you studied the seven types of spiders found in South America or identified the five key battles of the American Revolutionary War.

In college, you must become more than just a passive absorber of information. You will need to actively participate in your own education by processing information into knowledge. Having knowledge about a subject means you can demonstrate and understand key facts and broad concepts. It means you can integrate new knowledge with prior knowledge, and apply your knowledge to other situations. In short, you have an interrelated network of knowledge in your mind rather than just a list of facts you can repeat. In essence, you are a critical thinker who can operate at all six levels of Bloom's taxonomy of the cognitive domain.

Many college students have a hard time distinguishing between memorization and knowledge, since college courses require elements of both. Introductory courses in the sciences and mathematics rely more heavily on memorization, so you can develop a foundation of information on which to build an understanding of the disciplines. On the other hand, beginning courses in the liberal arts typically require you to understand and analyze broad concepts so you can build a foundation for further study in the field.

THE DIFFERENCE BETWEEN EDUCATION AND TRAINING

As you move to higher-level courses in all areas of study, you will progress to a greater emphasis on knowledge. You will be expected to think rather than merely generate "the right answer." Thinking progresses from "What is the right answer?" to "How do I get to the right answer?" to "Why is this the right answer?"

This progression is the difference between training and education. Training enables you to generate the right answer only in a given situation. A good example of training is a mathematical formula. If you have been trained well, all you need to know is what type of problem you are facing and then remember

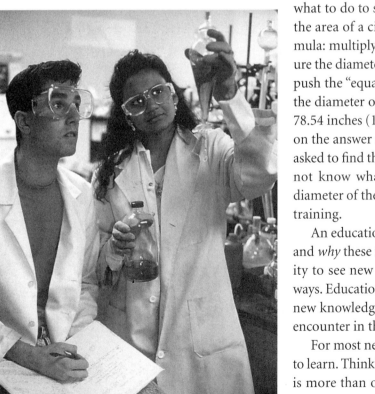

what to do to solve it. For example, if you are asked to give the area of a circle, you need to remember the proper formula: multiply the square of the diameter by 0.7854, measure the diameter, enter the information into your calculator, push the "equals" button, and you have the right answer. If the diameter of a circle is 10 inches, the area of the circle is 78.54 inches ($10^2 \times 0.7854$). If your answer matches the one on the answer sheet, you get full credit. However, if you are asked to find the circumference of that same circle, you may not know what to do unless the formula (multiply the diameter of the circle by pi, or 3.1416) was included in your training.

An education takes you beyond training to learning *how* and *why* these formulas work. Education gives you the ability to see new relationships and apply knowledge in new ways. Education enables you to solve problems and generate new knowledge to meet the unforeseen situations you will encounter in the future.

For most new college students, this is a new, exciting way to learn. Thinking at higher levels and recognizing that there is more than one way to learn will open up new learning opportunities for you. When you really start learning and gaining knowledge, you will increase your potential for success in college and in life.

▲ *Everyone Does Not Learn the Same Way*

Almost all students have subjects that come easily for them and others that are a constant challenge. For some, English and history courses are a breeze; for others, the sciences are the easiest. The reason for this difference is that people learn differently. Each of us has our own learning style. Understanding your personal learning style is important. Knowing how you learn best can affect your success in a course and help you choose a major and career. Students generally do best with instructors whose learning styles most closely match their own. They also excel in majors and careers that match their learning styles.

You have probably noticed a difference between the way your math professor teaches and the way your English professor teaches. They may approach their subjects, teaching, and worlds very differently because of differences in individual learning styles.

You also may find professors in the same subject who have radically different teaching styles. Two professors may use the same book and teach from the same outline but emphasize different points and test for different purposes. One professor may emphasize facts and figures and use all multiple-choice and true-false questions to test your recall of the facts. The other may emphasize general concepts and use multiple-choice, problem, and essay questions to test your understanding of the concepts and how to apply them. Similarly, your approach to learning will differ between the two classes. You may do well with one professor and poorly with the other, depending on how well your learning style matches that of the professor.

If you know your learning style and have a choice of professors, you should choose the one whose learning style most closely matches your own so you can increase your chances for a better grade. First, you need to understand your own learning style and be able to recognize the learning styles of your professors.

DISCOVERING YOUR LEARNING STYLE

Your learning style is a combination of how you perceive and how you process information. Remember, there is no one best way to think and learn. What works best for you depends on the situation. Since you will face a variety of learning situations every day, it is important for you to be comfortable with more than one learning style.

One aspect of your learning style is *how you perceive reality*. Researchers in this area separate people into two general groups. The first group relies heavily on sensing, feeling, and intuition to understand reality. This approach usually works best in unstructured situations. The second group relies heavily on facts and logic to understand reality. This group takes a more clinical, scientific approach that usually works best in structured situations. This style leaves little room for emotion.

The processing part of your learning style deals with *how you internalize information* once you acquire it and how you make it your own. Again, researchers have placed people into two general groups. The first group wants to jump right in and begin using the newly acquired information right away. The second group wants to observe and review the new information before starting to use it. The following exercise can help you determine which learning style or styles best apply to you.

ACTIVE LEARNING

Exercise 9.1 *By using the Internet, you can take a learning styles test on your own and have your responses analyzed online. The advantage of this approach is that you can take the test in private anytime and receive the results quickly.*

To take the test, called the Keirsey-Bates Indicator, go to the following web site:

http://www.keirsey.com

There are no right or wrong answers to these questions. It is what you learn about yourself that matters. Most people find that their learning style is a combination of styles rather than a pure version of any single style. Your results may also vary depending on when and under what circumstances you take the test.

After you have taken the test and received the analysis of your responses, investigate the other links at that site to gain a better appreciation of what these results do and do not mean for you.

On a separate sheet of paper, describe in writing your preferred learning style. What did you learn about yourself from this exercise? What is the most surprising thing you learned? The least surprising thing? How accurately do you think this test described your preferred approach to learning?

▲ Mind Mapping

Mind mapping, the process of diagramming what you are learning, is a valuable approach because it encourages you to be more than a passive absorber of information. You must be an active listener, observer, and thinker. You must be able to link pieces of new information together in a logical way that accurately reflects what you are learning. To do this, you must first perceive the new information correctly and then process it in a way that makes sense. In essence,

you make the information your own. Once you can do this, you are on your way to becoming a critical thinker. This is a giant step toward making a successful transition from high school to college learning.

Teachers often disassemble their personal mind map of a subject or concept and then transfer it to their students, who assemble a similar mind map of the material in their own minds. Comparing mind maps of several students in a class with the one drawn by the professor often yields interesting results. Some mind maps may be identical, whereas others show different levels of comprehension.

One way to draw a mind map is to start with a blank sheet of paper and write the topic at the center, then draw a circle around it. Draw lines out from the center idea—like the spokes of a wheel—and put sub-ideas at the ends of the spokes. Then put a circle around each sub-idea and, from each sub-idea, branch out again with spokes and write several sub-sub-ideas. Continue until you have all your ideas down on paper and all the concepts properly connected to one another.

Mind maps can take on many different formats, such as a time line, a cause-and-effect chart or picture, a graph, or some other visual representation. Remember to be creative and accurate as you visually depict ideas and concepts. Figure 9.1 is a mind map for this chapter drawn by the authors.

COLLABORATIVE LEARNING

Exercise 9.2 *On a separate sheet of paper, draw your own mind map for this chapter. When you are done, compare it with the one the authors drew in Figure 9.1. How are they similar? How are they different? Break up into groups of three or four and discuss the similarities and the differences among group members' mind maps and the one drawn by the authors.*

FIGURE 9.1 Mind Map

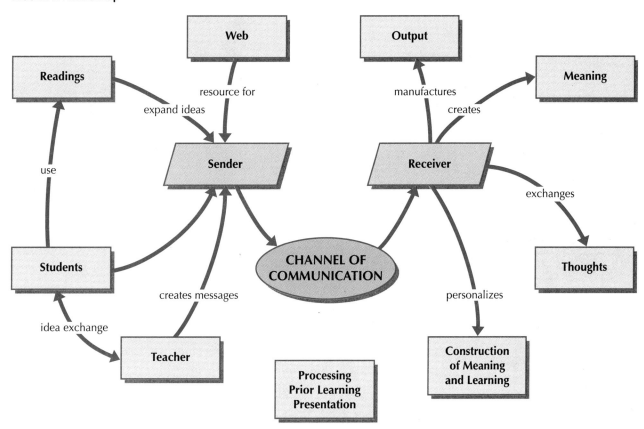

CRITICAL THINKING

Exercise 9.3 *Bring to class an article from a recent newspaper or news magazine (e.g.,* Time, Newsweek*) that discusses a world event or government decision. On a separate piece of paper, draw a mind map of the article (use something other than the circles and spokes mentioned earlier). Be prepared to explain your mind map to the class.*

CRITICAL THINKING

Exercise 9.4 *The U.S. Constitution states that individuals must be 30 years old to become a U.S senator. On a separate sheet of paper, defend this age requirement in a short essay using all levels of Bloom's taxonomy of cognitive learning.*

CRITICAL THINKING

Exercise 9.5 *Suppose you recently inherited $1 million from a distant relative. Describe how you would prioritize your spending of the money. Then depict your priority list as a mind map. List your top ten expenditures and defend your choices.*

ETHICS

Exercise 9.6 *Recently your local representative to the U.S. Congress stepped down from office for personal reasons. You are elected to fill the rest of the term. The former representative was an avid supporter of the National Rifle Association. You also believe strongly in the right to bear arms. However, a small group of your constituents makes a strong argument for more gun control. In a public meeting, members of this group ask you to support their gun control program. As the new* representative, how would you respond to the 2,000 constituents in attendance at this public meeting?

_____

_____

_____

_____

_____

CRITICAL THINKING

Exercise 9.7 *Find out what the organizational relationship is between your professors and your school's administration. On a separate sheet of paper, draw a chart showing how your entire school is organized.*

CRITICAL THINKING

Exercise 9.8 *What is the function of your school's undergraduate student government? Explain in a short paragraph how your student government operates. Then create a mind map of its organizational structure.*

CRITICAL THINKING

Exercise 9.9 *What do you think would happen if your campus banned all alcohol? Predict the two most likely outcomes. What is your position on this ban? Be prepared to discuss your position in class. (Expect a lively debate on this topic.)*

_____

_____

_____

_____

ACTIVE LEARNING

Exercise 9.10 *Create a plan for involving students in extracurricular activities. On a separate sheet of paper, identify at least three suggestions for implementing your plan in a memo to be sent to your school's administration.*

ACTIVE LEARNING

Exercise 9.11 *On a separate sheet of paper, write a three-paragraph essay describing how you can apply three new attitudes to your thinking.*

CRITICAL THINKING

Exercise 9.12 *Evaluate one full week of your classes and think of instances where you were challenged to be a critical thinker. On a separate sheet of paper, write a paragraph describing at least three of these situations.*

CRITICAL THINKING

Exercise 9.13 *Choose one chapter of one of your college texts. Identify specific areas in the chapter where the author uses the different levels of Bloom's taxonomy.*

CHAPTER HIGHLIGHTS

1. The proper attitude is important for learning.

2. The three elements of a good attitude are open-mindedness, whole-heartedness, and responsibility.

3. Critical thinking can be developed through good questioning because it shows where you are on Bloom's taxonomy of the cognitive domain.

4. Critical thinkers can differentiate between opinions and facts.

5. Your memory is separated into short-term and long-term memory. Items in your short-term memory are quickly forgotten. Items that move into your long-term memory remain there for a long time, and sometimes indefinitely.

6. Repetition of information is the primary factor that moves information into long-term memory.

7. Information that is taken in as part of an all-night cramming session goes only into short-term memory and is soon lost.

8. Memorization requires little learning. Knowledge means you have built an interrelated network of information that you can integrate with prior knowledge and apply to other situations.

9. There are differences between training and education. Training gives you the ability to discover the right answer. Education enables you to understand the *how* and the *why* behind the answers. An education not only allows you to help solve today's problems but also equips you to generate new knowledge in the future.

10. Your learning style is the combination of how you perceive and how you process information.

11. Not everyone learns the same way. Each of us has a different learning style.

12. Your learning style can affect the grade you receive in a course and your choice of a career or major.

13. People generally do best in majors and careers that match their learning styles.

14. You can do better in a course if you understand the learning style of your professor.

15. Mind mapping gives you a visual way to understand and arrange what you learn.

CASE STUDY
Jim's Roller Coaster Grades

As everyone else rushed to the front of the classroom to get their first economics exam back from Professor Weaver, Jim held back. He was sure he had not done well on the test. He was surprised that in a course with 250 students, the test had been all essay questions and problems. Since Professor Weaver was new, Jim had no way of knowing what kind of test she would give. Jim had looked at the old exams from Professor Dunn, who had taught this class before Professor Weaver. All of his exams were multiple-choice and true-false questions. If this was the same course, why were the exams so different?

Economics and English were the only courses Jim was struggling with this first semester. Things were going really well in chemistry, biology, and math. He liked these courses because they did not get emotional about their subject or ask him how he felt about some poem or picture. He enjoyed the sciences because things were clear-cut. All he had to do was report what he saw. His mother had been right when she said he had a real flair for science. She was the one who suggested that he become a veterinarian. Last summer he had enjoyed working with their local veterinarian, Dr. Hutchinson, who had allowed him to assist in the diagnosis and treatment of several cases. Jim liked that he could quickly apply things he was learning from Dr. Hutchinson.

All his life, Jim had earned a reputation as the kind of person who never looked before he leaped. Those who knew him best, however, saw someone who always carefully sized up his situation and then moved quickly once he decided what to do. In high school, he was president of the computer club. After reading a few books on local area networks and spending a lot of time on the Internet, he and another student set up the school's PCs into a network so that everyone could have access to the school library's online card catalog without leaving the classroom. After this project, Jim admitted that he and his partner did not have everything worked out before they started. They spent half their time figuring out how to solve the unexpected problems they encountered along the way. Jim thought it was one of the greatest things he had ever done. He liked problems that had challenging solutions.

When Jim finally grabbed his economics test from the pile, he found that his hunch was right; he had a 68 percent with a note from the teaching assistant to see her. He would never get into veterinary school unless he did well in all his courses, even the ones that seemed unrelated to the profession. Jim was going to have to figure out why he did poorly on the test. He rarely missed class, and he had started studying three days before the test.

If Jim asked you for advice on how to study for exams in economics, what would you tell him?

Which of the learning styles found on the Keirsey-Bates Indicator (see Exercise 9.1) best describes Jim's learning style? Explain your answer. Is Jim's learning style best suited for being a veterinarian? Why or why not? If not, what majors would be best for him? Why?

If Jim were given a choice between Professors Weaver and Dunn for this course, which one should he choose? Why?

Personal Journal

CRITICAL THINKING

Personal Journal 9.1 Describe a course in which your learning style closely matches that of the professor. Describe a course where it does not. Explain what you are doing differently to succeed in the second course. Has the information in this chapter changed your approach to learning? If so, how? Describe how your self-awareness has changed since you began college. How are you better or worse off for the change?

_____

_____

_____

_____

_____

_____

_____

_____

_____

_____

DIVERSITY

Personal Journal 9.2 One of the major advantages of going to college is meeting people from a variety of backgrounds, religions, countries, cultures, and experiences. Describe how your view of the world has changed since you started college. Describe a particular experience that changed your perspective on the people of the world.

_____

_____

_____

_____

_____

_____

_____

_____

_____

CHAPTER QUIZ

1. Describe the different functions of the left and right lobes of the brain.

_____

_____

_____

_____

_____

2. Why do some people call college learning a "left-brained activity"?

_____

_____

_____

_____

3. Describe the process of moving information from short-term to long-term memory.

_____

_____

_____

_____

4. What is the difference between learning and memorization?

_____

_____

_____

_____

_____

5. What is the difference between education and training?

_____

_____

_____

_____

_____

6. What is a learning style?

_____

_____

_____

_____

7. How does mind mapping enhance your learning?

_____

_____

_____

_____

8. Why is your attitude important to being a good thinker?

_____

_____

_____

_____

_____

9. How do you know if an opinion is valid?

_____

_____

_____

_____

_____

ADDITIONAL RESOURCES

Ackoff, Russell L. *The Art of Problem Solving, Accompanied by Ackoff's Fables.* New York: John Wiley & Sons, 1978.

Dewey, John. *How We Think: A Restatement of the Relationship of Reflective Thinking to the Educative Process.* Lexington, MA: D. C. Heath and Company, 1933.

Gelb, Michael J. *How to Think Like Leonardo da Vinci.* New York: Delacorte Press, 1998.

CHAPTER 10

Finding the Right Major and Career

CHAPTER OBJECTIVES

After reading this chapter, you will understand why:

- Your academic adviser is an important part of your academic and career planning.
- Choosing a major is a process.
- You must assume responsibility in selecting a major and planning a career.
- Assessing your career goals helps you develop your academic plan.
- There is a relationship between experiential learning and academics.
- You need a winning résumé.
- Campus career services can be a key ingredient in your career planning.

After reading this chapter, you will know how to:

- Work with your adviser to help you reach your academic and career goals.
- Develop important questions to ask yourself and your adviser about potential careers and majors.
- Expand your sources of academic information related to majors.
- Validate your choice of a major.
- Search for, find, and secure employment opportunities while still in school.

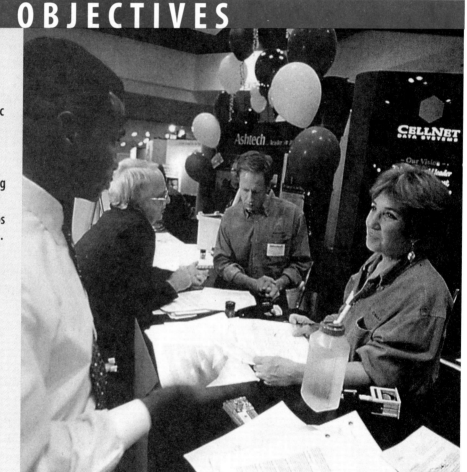

You most likely will recall when, as a child, you proudly announced your plans to become a doctor, a lawyer, a scientist, a teacher, or something else. Whatever career you chose, you probably knew about it from a family member, a television program, or a book. During elementary school, you likely expanded your job possibilities and began to understand the role education would play in qualifying you for an occupation. In high school, you were encouraged to clarify your career plans. Perhaps you talked to career counselors or experienced a career day to help you set your goals. Your high school library may have had several shelves of books for you to explore different occupations. Despite all this help, now that you are in college, you may find yourself with no clear career goals and no idea of what major to choose.

This dilemma is not unusual, however. Most students enter college with only a vague idea of where they are headed. Most change their majors and career goals several times during their college years. College is a great place to sort out your career goals. A college education is a learning process whereby you develop your sense of self-awareness and begin to think for yourself. It is a process of discovery in which you learn many things about yourself, including your abilities and your likes and dislikes. As you learn more about yourself, you will discover new choices unfolding and new opportunities to explore.

▲ Not as Easy as It Looks

You have completed at least 12 years of school, you have been a successful student, and your family respects your maturity and ability to make good decisions. Your teachers rewarded you for completing high-quality work in a timely fashion. Your extracurricular activities were viewed as valuable contributions to your school and community. In high school, you had a sense of pride, confidence, and respect as a good student. The idea of selecting a major and a career seemed straightforward since you had handled everything up until now without much effort.

Now you find yourself in a world that is unlike anything you have ever experienced. You may be far from home, sharing a small room with a total stranger. You met with your college adviser for about 15 minutes, and she or he helped you select your courses for this semester. Although the adviser was polite and helpful, you did not get the same comfortable feeling that you did when you talked to your favorite high school teacher, whom you knew well. On the basis of the first few weeks of college, you are having second thoughts about your chosen career in, say, microbiology or English literature. Meanwhile your roommate is bubbling with confidence about becoming a graphic artist. Something seems all wrong.

Relax. You are not alone. These are normal feelings for first-year students. One reason you came to college was to understand who you are and what you want to be. Now it's time to push yourself outside your comfort zone and look for the answers to these questions. You will not discover all the answers in one day or even in one year; your plan will take time and effort to evolve. Some college students like the idea of having their whole life mapped out for them well in advance. Others prefer to explore all of their possibilities before they commit to a specific goal.

Think for a moment about who knows you best. Of course, you probably know yourself best. You have been making your own decisions, you work and earn your own money, and you can vote. But this does not mean that you have to make this journey by yourself. Your school has advisers, counselors, and others who can help you make good decisions. They can help you discover and nurture your talents and skills, and match them to the best career for you.

▲ Assessing Your Career Goals

When choosing a career, you should first examine your academic interests. What courses did you like most in high school? Be sure to consider carefully whether you liked the subject or whether you liked or disliked the teacher (see Exercise 10.1). Begin to think about your favorite subjects and the people who taught them. Ask yourself whether you make choices based on external forces or whether you look into yourself to make decisions. Do you allow others to decide for you, or do you consider the opinions of others only as resources to help you make informed decisions for yourself?

CRITICAL THINKING

Exercise 10.1

1. List your six favorite courses completed in high school. Rank the courses from 1 to 6, with 1 being your most favorite course and 6 your least favorite. Identify the last name of the teacher who taught each course, then rank the teachers from most to least favorite.

	Course	Ranking	Teacher	Ranking
1.				
2.				
3.				
4.				
5.				
6.				

2. Based on your rankings, answer the following questions:

   a. What aspects of your top three courses did you like most? Choose an adjective that best describes each course (for example, *interesting, challenging, rigorous*).

   b. What characteristics of your top three teachers did you like most? Choose an adjective that best describes each one (for example, *enthusiastic, professional, funny, smart*).

3. Consider how other people, such as teachers, friends, and family members, have influenced your choices about such things as academic subjects, books, movies, hobbies, and careers. Then answer the following questions:

   a. Why did you choose this college? Who influenced your choice?

   b. Why did you choose each of your classes? Who influenced your choices?

   c. Identify one choice you have made recently to please someone else.

4. Recall again your career thoughts as a young child. What did you want to be when you grew up? In a small group, discuss why you changed your mind or why you decided to still pursue that career. Summarize the main things in your life that have influenced your career choice, and share them with group members.

While you are in college, you will constantly examine your academic interests, abilities, and opportunities. First, consider whether your academic interests

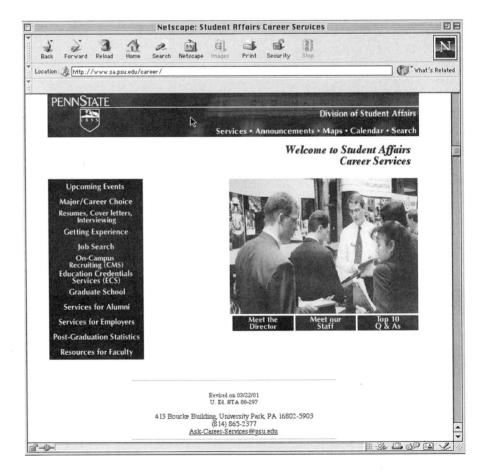

are realistic given your preparation and abilities. Find out if your college offers a major that meets your career goals (see Exercise 10.2).

ACTIVE LEARNING

Exercise 10.2 *Visit a career counselor on your campus. Identify and list six specific resources and services available in your career center.*

ACTIVE LEARNING

Exercise 10.3 *Answer the following questions:*

1. What career do you want to pursue when you finish your education?
2. How do you intend to pursue that career? Be specific.
3. List three career resources you can use to learn more about your career choice.

Now discuss your academic and career plans with a family member or a close friend. What are their opinions? Do they have any suggestions that you can use to implement your plans?

▲ Experiential Learning

Career awareness includes a systematic plan to examine what possibilities exist for you to contribute to the working world. Standardized tests such as the **Jackson Career Interest Inventory Test** provide some insights, but should not be used as a "crystal ball." These written tests help you match the characteristics

of specific careers with your preferences and abilities. They help you pinpoint occupations in which you might find a great deal of career satisfaction and success. These tests do not guarantee the ideal choices, but they can be good tools to help you make informed decisions (see Exercise 10.4).

ACTIVE LEARNING

Exercise 10.4 *Visit your career services office and ask if it administers the Jackson Career Interest Inventory Test. If it is available, arrange to take the test. Then write a paragraph describing what you learned from taking the test. What surprised you most? What surprised you least? Return to your academic adviser to see if your academic plans are consistent with your career goals.*

Career exploration is the next step in determining your career goals. As you explore different careers, you will need to ask many questions of individuals who are involved in the career you are considering (see Exercise 10.5). A good way to accomplish this is to visit a business or an industry that employs people in your career field. Some may offer a formalized **externship** that allows you to follow an employee who does the job you are exploring. Some externships last for just one day; others go for a week or longer. Some colleges give academic credit for externships. Even if you do not earn college credit for this work, it is a great way to learn about a potential career.

ACTIVE LEARNING

Exercise 10.5

1. On a separate sheet of paper, make a list of ten careers you are considering.
2. Next to each career, identify a college major that supports your career goal.

3. Interview one person involved in each of the ten careers and identify the specific academic path he or she followed to prepare for that career.

Many colleges offer planned, supervised, educational work experiences related to various majors that allow students to try out a job in their career of interest. Such **career capstone experiences** may include an *internship* or a *cooperative education work experience.*

In an **internship** you work full-time for an employer, usually for one semester. You, the employer, and a faculty adviser work together to plan your work experience. The employer agrees to guide you through a work experience that exposes you to all the tasks that full-time workers in this area do every day. These tasks are fully explained and agreed on in writing before you begin to work. The faculty member coordinates and approves the work experience for credit. When you have completed the internship, you write a report describing what you did and what you learned from the experience. The employer evaluates your performance and recommends to the faculty member what grade you should receive for the work.

A **cooperative education work experience** is similar to an internship. In this arrangement, you alternate between semesters of college course work and employment as a regular part of your degree program.

ACTIVE LEARNING

Exercise 10.6

1. Interview a cooperative education coordinator. Determine the requirements for applying for a cooperative education work experience. How long does the arrangement last—one semester, one year? Do you choose your employer? How much credit do you earn for this experience? Are you paid for your work?

2. Interview a student who has completed a cooperative education work experience. Ask about the value of the experience and whether it led the student to alter his or her choice of major.

It is never too soon to begin exploring experiential learning. By the time you graduate, you may have experienced several externships, internships, or cooperative education opportunities offered by your college. You may also want to explore some creative types of experiential learning activities offered by other colleges and universities. Some institutions offer international internships that are available to students studying in other colleges. Find out if the activity will delay your graduation by a semester or two. If it will, you may find the delay to be time well spent if it helps you clarify and accomplish your career objectives. To make this kind of decision, you may need to do a personal cost/benefit analysis to decide if this experience is worthwhile for you (see Exercise 10.7).

ACTIVE LEARNING

Exercise 10.7

Cost/Benefit Analysis

1. Will the experiential activity help me clarify my choice of a major? If so, how?

2. How likely is the experience to lead to full-time employment and a better salary when I graduate?

3. Will the activity help me get a scholarship award?

4. Does the experience pay a salary?

5. Will the experience delay my graduation? If so, would I consider it time well spent?

▲ Creating a Résumé

A résumé is a document that introduces you to an employer for whom you would like to work. You need a résumé to explain your educational background, work experiences, personal information, references, job objective, and special skills. Your résumé should be concise and accurately reflect your talents and experience. It should also convince a potential employer that you will contribute something to the organization.

In addition to your résumé, an effective cover letter that accompanies the résumé gives you another opportunity to introduce yourself to a potential employer. The cover letter should be brief and concise, but should contain two or three notable items about you. It should highlight a particular strength you have that an employer might value. An effective cover letter also showcases your ability to write and clearly express your ideas.

A good word-processing program will produce a professional-looking résumé and cover letter. If you do not have access to a computer, use a very good typewriter. Check your documents carefully for grammatical, spelling, and word usage errors.

ACTIVE LEARNING   **Exercise 10.8**

1. Create a one-page résumé that includes your present work and educational experiences.

2. Presume it is ten years from now. Create a one-page résumé that includes your projected work and educational experiences at that time. Write a convincing cover letter highlighting a particular strength of yours that would benefit the organization.

3. Break up into small groups and share your résumés and cover letters. Share suggestions for improvement among group members.

4. Write a paragraph explaining how you plan to achieve the accomplishments highlighted in your résumé of the future.

▲ Academic Planning and Goal Setting

As you saw in the first two chapters of this book, goals help you focus your energy. When you decide to pursue a particular career, you have set a goal—a target to aim for. Your next step is to translate this career goal into an appropriate major that will permit you to accomplish it. Then identify the majors at your college that best prepare you to meet your career goal.

Lisa Senior
335 West Beaver Avenue
State College, PA 16801
Email: lxs@psu.edu
Phone: (814) 231-000X

OBJECTIVE: To obtain a position in the field of Information Technology, specific interest in SAP.

EDUCATION: Pennsylvania State University, University Park, PA
Bachelor of Science in Management Science and Information Systems
Expected graduation date: May 2000
Major GPA: 3.24/4.0

Relevant Courses:

| *Mathematical Programming* | *Statistical Analysis* | *Forecasting* |
| *Economics* | *Accounting* | *Business Writing* |

EXPERIENCE: **Johnson & Johnson**   **January XX – May XX**
Logistics Analyst
- Managed automated order processing to allow International customers to order directly via EDI or FTP.
- Managed the Vendor Managed Inventory (VMI) for Global Affiliates to reduce and maintain their on-hand inventory.
- Responsible for running weekly orders and ensuring at the beginning of every month that the database was updated with the new forecasts and new safety stocks measurements if any.
- Responsible for analyzing International forecasts and supporting the creation of a web page to be posted on the Johnson & Johnson Intranet.
- Assisted in the Global Air-Freight Data collection Project (GAP) to reconsider Johnson & Johnson freight carriers and their rates.

Pennsylvannia State University   **August XX – Present**
Tutor, University Learning Center
- Currently tutoring students in
  – Financial and Managerial Accounting for Decision Making
  – Introductory Microeconomics Analysis and Policy
- Completed University Learning Center certification process.

SKILLS: **Computer**
- Worked extensively with simulation programming languages such as Excel and ARENA
- Professionally trained in Mercia Lincs (CRP system), MGF/Pro (Manufacturing, Planning, and Costing system), and in COACT (Order Processing System)
- Maintenance of Database Management systems

ACTIVITIES: *President, Asian American Student Caucus*
- Led the weekly meetings and organized various events throughout the semester
Secretary of Alpha Beta Chi service/social sorority
- Organized participation in AIDS walk and Diabetes walk as well as visits to a local nursing facility in State College, PA
Operations Committee member for Penn State Dance Marathon

REFERENCES: Available Upon Request.

ACTIVE LEARNING

Exercise 10.9 *What career goal have you chosen to pursue at this point? (If you have not chosen one, take this opportunity to pinpoint a career that most closely matches your interests.) Use your school's general catalog to answer the following questions about your career:*

1. Identify six majors offered at your college that relate to your career goal.

2. Explain why these six majors are of interest to you.

3. Identify one concern you have about each major you are exploring.

4. Write a paragraph describing each course you are taking this semester. How does each course fit into the majors you are considering? How will your courses help you accomplish your career goal?

SELECTING AN ADVISER

When you enrolled in college, an academic adviser was most likely assigned to you. The assignment was based on your expected major as stated on your application for admission. Your adviser may be either a professional academic adviser or a faculty member. She or he understands the college's policies and procedures as well as the goals of its academic programs. Your adviser has access to your academic records, such as high school transcripts, SAT or ACT scores, and placement test scores. These records tell your adviser a great deal about you and your abilities, but they reveal nothing about your life, your career goals, your personal situation, how college is changing the way you think, or countless other things that make you who you are. To really get to know you, your adviser needs to talk with you one-on-one.

Your academic adviser can help you think critically about the numerous opportunities that will help you reach your goals. Your adviser can help you design an academic plan that fits your interests and abilities, and encourage you to consider a variety of life and career goals. If your adviser is unavailable or uninformed about a specific question, seek additional help. It is important that you be proactive in obtaining information and formulating your plan. Ask questions of faculty members, career counselors, administrators, family, friends, or others who can help. Try asking many people the same questions to get a variety of responses. Use the library and the Internet to supplement your information. Finally, you should sit down by yourself, review all the information you have gathered, and make a decision.

PREPARING YOUR QUESTIONS

You will want to ask several questions about possible majors. Many schools admit students only to a college and not to a major until later. Your first adviser may be an individual who has a broad background that will help you sort out your life and career goals. This person will also know about the variety of majors your school offers, what prerequisites are needed, how many semesters each major takes, and possible employment opportunities related to each major, including beginning salaries. Your adviser can help you find answers to a host of questions, such as: (1) What can I do with a liberal arts degree? (2) Do I need to complete all my math classes before I start taking upper-level engineering classes? (3) To become a medical doctor, should I major in biology or take a specialized pre-med program?

ACTIVE LEARNING

Exercise 10.10 *A Weekly Advice Collection Box is an exercise that can help you to formally set a career goal and identify the majors at your school that are most compatible with that goal. Your weekly contributions to the Advice Collection Box will consist of your responses in Figure 10.1.*

FIGURE 10.1 **Advice Collection Box**

Week # _____

Date   _____

   1. I will meet with _____ (person) to discuss

     _____ (topic or question) on _____

     (time and date) at _____ (location).

   2. Advice given:

     _____

     _____

   3. I will write a one-page summary describing what I learned from my meeting.

   4. I will follow up my meeting by doing these activities:

     _____

     _____

     _____

   5. I will do the following activities next week in anticipation of my next meeting that will add another question and solution to my Advice Collection Box.

     _____

     _____

     _____

   6. I will discuss my progress with _____ (a friend

     or family member) on _____ (time and date).

After contributing to your advice box for at least six weeks, evaluate your progress. What career goal most interests you at this point? What majors best match this goal? If you have not come to a comfortable career goal decision, continue adding to your advice box.

COLLABORATIVE LEARNING

Exercise 10.11 *Select three of the majors from your list in Exercise 10.9. For each major, determine what employment opportunities might be possible. Pair up with a classmate and compare your findings.*

Once you have narrowed down your list of majors to about three, it is time to begin a more in-depth investigation. A good start is to talk with the faculty member in charge of each major that interests you. This information is usually available in the college's general catalog or on its web page. Then phone or email that person to request an appointment. During your initial contact, explain the purpose of your visit and ask if there is information that you can pick up before your meeting. Examining this material ahead of time will help you develop better questions. Your questions may include: What kind of employment do graduates in this major usually find? What percentage of graduates find work in their area of study within six months of graduation? How long does it take to complete the program? Do most students participate in internships? Do you have to earn a graduate degree to find work in this discipline?

Another way to get a feel for what a major entails is to join clubs and other organizations related to that discipline. By joining these groups, you will meet other people who are actively involved in the program. Ask students why they are enrolled in this major and what they hope to achieve by getting a degree in this area. Ask about different classes and the faculty members who teach them. Are the professors open to questions, and are they available to help you both in and out of class? What are the job prospects like for graduates in this field?

Your investigation should also include examining the supplemental activities that come with each major, such as a minor or an additional area of specialization, internship or externship opportunities, participation in research projects, serving as a teaching assistant, or enrolling in education-abroad programs. Each of these activities offers you a chance to enrich your college experience and enhance your job prospects after graduation. They also give you opportunities to experience firsthand the career you are planning.

ACTIVE LEARNING

Exercise 10.12

1. From your list in Exercise 10.9, identify one major that most appeals to you. Interview a faculty member in that program.

2. Write a two-paragraph summary of what you learned, including the professor's education, career goals, research activities, and published articles and books. Report your findings to your class.

3. Obtain and read a publication written by this faculty member. Write a one-paragraph summary of what you read.

4. Summarize in one paragraph how this faculty member's research or career path has changed in the past ten years.

▲ *Your Major: Is It 'Til Death Do You Part?*

Commitment is an extraordinary word. Keeping our promises to others and to ourselves is something we all value. Yet sometimes change is good. Let's look at a student named Shari. Since she was a child, Shari had dreamed of becoming a nurse. Six other members of her family, including her brother and a cousin, are nurses, and Shari expected to follow their paths. But after two semesters of college, and despite good grades, Shari knew that a nursing career was not for her, and she began to explore other majors. Now Shari thinks she wants to be a civil engineer (although there are no engineers in her family). During the school year, she got to know some engineering students and faculty members through her roommate, who is an engineering major. In addition, she has attended several student engineering club meetings. On the basis of this information, she knows that civil engineering will be her new major.

Changing majors in college is not something you should do casually, but you should feel free to do it when appropriate. In Shari's case, careful investigation made it clear that her talents and interests were in engineering and not nursing. Grades were not an issue. Finding a career and a major that meets her needs will spare her from an unhappy stint in her "expected" profession.

To make this switch, Shari must do several things. First, she needs to ask whether she can switch to another major, since some schools admit students into one specific program. Assuming she can switch, Shari next needs to speak with an engineering adviser to find out if she qualifies for the civil engineering program. If she does not, she must find out what she needs to do to qualify (she may even have to transfer to another school). Third, Shari needs to ask how many of the credits she has already completed can be applied to the requirements for a degree in civil engineering. Since most freshmen take introductory courses that meet the university's general education requirements, the courses she has taken probably can be applied to her new degree requirements. Fourth, Shari will find out that an engineering degree often requires as many as 30 more credits to graduate. This could keep her in school for an extra year—but that is a small price to pay for finding her life's work.

STUDENT RESPONSIBILITIES FOR ACADEMIC ADVISING

Since an academic adviser is unlikely to seek you out, you need to take the major responsibility for your own academic advising. Most institutions send their students all the information they need and assign them an academic adviser, but the rest is up to you. You must take the initiative to schedule regular appointments with your adviser to discuss your progress, clarify your degree and career plans, make course selections, and plan your course sequencing. By graduation, you will have met and discussed your academic plans with many faculty members and academic advisers.

For academic advising to work, you must be an active participant in the process. Since you are the only one who can decide your future, you should be constantly conducting self-evaluations to know where you are headed. At any moment, you should be able to answer the following questions:

- Why am I majoring in _____ (name of major)?

- Why am I *not* majoring in _____ (a major of interest to you)?

- How am I doing in each of my classes?

- Why am I doing well in my _____ class?

- Why am I *not* doing well in my _____ class?

- What are my academic objectives for this semester?

- What are my long-run academic objectives?

- What progress did I make toward meeting my academic objectives last week?

- What am I doing next week to meet my academic objectives?

- Who is my academic adviser?

- When was the last time I talked with my academic adviser?

- Name three students who are enrolled in my academic major.

Having good answers to these questions helps you to stay on target to reach your academic goals. The questions are not a test; they are for your benefit. The questions enhance your self-awareness and keep you focused on achieving your life goals.

ACTIVE LEARNING   **Exercise 10.13** *Using the chart in Figure 10.2, list all the faculty members, coun-selors, and others with whom you have discussed or should have discussed your career goals and possible majors.*

FIGURE 10.2 **Career Planning Reference List**

Name	Title	Department	Address	Phone	Email	Contact Date

CHAPTER HIGHLIGHTS

1. Being a college student involves more than classroom preparation.

2. Three levels of experiential learning include awareness, exploration, and a capstone planned, supervised, educational work experience.

3. You should determine the costs and benefits of participating in an experiential learning experience.

4. Experiential learning activities can relate directly to full-time employment upon graduation.

5. Many resources exist to help college students clarify career interests, including career services offices, career counselors, academic advisers, and faculty members.

6. Constructing academic and career goals is a valuable activity. You will benefit from periodically reflecting on and discussing your goals with others.

CHAPTER HIGHLIGHTS

CASE STUDY
Jennifer's Big Leap

Jennifer always said she wanted to be a scientist, or maybe a medical doctor, or a laboratory researcher for a big pharmaceutical company like the one her father works for. Her first semester in college focused on calculus, chemistry, biology, and political science. By the end of that semester, she felt uncomfortable with the sciences. This was partly because she was earning less than the *A* grades she had always earned in high school. In fact, a *C+* grade point average at the end of her first semester suggested that she should forget a future career in the scientific community. The *A* grade she received in political science indicated that the social sciences might be the best choice for her major.

During spring break, Jennifer spoke to her father about her reluctance to pursue a degree in one of the sciences. He responded sternly that she should not quit her long-time goal. Her mother encouraged her to make up her own mind without feeling pressured by others to decide on a major or a future career. Confused by these different responses, Jennifer decided she would postpone choosing a major this semester. During the summer she would get a job as a server in a restaurant in her hometown so that she could think about choosing a major and finance her extra expenses for the fall semester. She believed her parents' generosity in paying for her tuition, room and board, and books should not include extras such as movies, pizza, and football games. Clueless about a choice of major, she would resume her decision making when she returned to college in the fall.

Is Jennifer making a good decision about waiting until her second year in college to decide about a major or a career? Why or why not? What should she do to make a wise choice for her major?

Personal Journal

SELF-AWARENESS

Personal Journal 10.1 Describe how your search for a major and a career has changed since you began college. What things have helped you get a better idea of what you want to do with your life? What are you going to do this semester to help you choose your major? If you have an academic adviser, have you met with him or her? If so, how helpful is this person?

_____

_____

_____

_____

_____

_____

_____

_____

_____

DIVERSITY

Personal Journal 10.2 Explain the following statement: "A 'glass ceiling' exists that prevents women from rising to the top positions in industry and government." Write a short essay explaining why you agree or disagree with this statement.

_____

_____

_____

_____

_____

_____

_____

_____

_____

CHAPTER QUIZ

1. Define *experiential learning*.

_____

_____

_____

_____

_____

2. How does experiential learning complement your formal education?

_____

_____

_____

_____

_____

3. What is the value of constructing a résumé projecting your skills and job qualifications ten years from now?

_____

_____

_____

_____

_____

4. List five resources that would help your career planning.

_____

_____

_____

_____

_____

5. When is the ideal time to begin planning your career?

_____

_____

_____

_____

_____

6. How do career plans, selection of a college major, and semester course selections all fit together?

_____

_____

_____

_____

_____

ADDITIONAL RESOURCES

Equal Opportunity Publications. *Women Engineer Magazine.* Published three times per year.

Hispanic Publishing Corporation. *Hispanic Magazine.* Published monthly.

Kalt, Neil C. *Career Power.* Pound Ridge, NY: Career Power Books, 1996.

National Association of Colleges and Employers. *Job Choices.* Published annually.

National Association of Colleges and Employers. *Job Choices in Business Magazine.* Published annually.

National Association of Colleges and Employers. *Job Choices in Science and Engineering.* Published annually.

Oakes, Elizabeth H., ed. *Career Exploration on the Internet.* Chicago: Ferguson Publishing, 1998.

CHAPTER 11

Personal Health

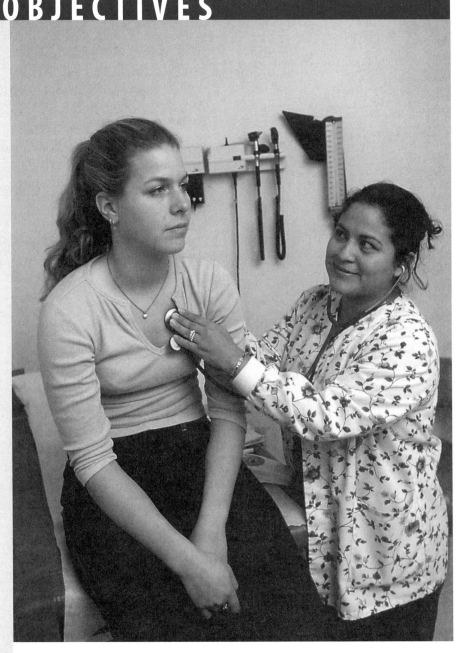

Success in college and in life is largely about personal responsibility and commitment. All the chapters so far have asked you to focus on how to apply these two principles directly to your classroom success. Now it is time to broaden your focus and apply personal responsibility and commitment to other parts of your life. These principles can also enable you to achieve a high level of success outside the classroom if you are physically and mentally prepared.

College is more than tests, books, and degrees. College-level learning enhances your ability to lead a happier, more productive, and healthier life. Because you have developed a strong sense of self-awareness, you can appreciate the benefits of keeping yourself in good physical and mental shape. When you are in good shape, you have the physical stamina and the mental toughness to undertake whatever is necessary to achieve your life goals. But to accomplish this means accepting personal responsibility for your own health and mental well-being and making a personal commitment to optimizing those areas of your life.

Success in life is about balance. People who have truly satisfying lives achieve successful careers while maintaining a happy family life and a wide circle of friends. They take the time to preserve their physical and mental health. They are involved in their community, religion, and a host of other areas that extend well beyond their jobs. A byproduct of a college education is that you develop a set of personal values defining who you are and how you relate to other people and to the world around you. This chapter discusses some of these issues so that *you* can decide what *your* approach to your health and well-being will be. After all, college is about being able to think for yourself and take responsibility for your choices. Although this chapter does not address all of the major issues you may face, it provides a good starting point. Feel free to add any other topics you think are needed.

▲ Stress, Nutrition, Exercise, and Sleep

The first group of topics deals with the common issues that confront us at all stages of life. As the pace of life quickens each day, you may tend to lose your perspective (self-awareness) about what is important to you and to your long-term health. You probably do not intend to lose your way, but somehow the urgent things simply overwhelm the things you normally consider important. When you give in to your urgent tasks, you may fail to realize how your decision affects your overall performance and your ability to achieve your life goals.

STRESS

Losing your way may start with something as simple as accepting your roommate's "urgent" challenge to play a new computer game. It is suddenly 11:00 P.M., and you still have to write your big chemistry lab report. You are forced to stay up until 3:00 A.M. to finish the report, which is probably not as good as the one you would have done if you had started it at 7:00 P.M. The next morning, you are too tired to make it to your early history class, which causes you to miss important information about next week's test. As a result, your grades in chemistry and history go down, which makes you fall below the minimum grade point average needed to get an interview for the job of your dreams. Now you are exhausted and overwhelmed with stress because you are not making progress toward your life goals. College is just filled with too much stress!

This example may seem a bit far-fetched, but nevertheless it makes a point. When you focus only on the "urgent" (playing a new computer game), you can lose sight of what is really important (achieving a life goal). This makes your life more stress filled because you are constantly busy but are making no progress toward the things you value most. However, if you maintain your perspective and work first on the things that are truly important to you, you will feel less stress in your life. You will not feel so overwhelmed, and you will know you are making progress toward your life goals.

Attending college is naturally a stressful event in your life, whatever your age or personal situation. You are now consistently being pushed out of your "comfort zone" and bombarded with new ideas, new subjects, new people, and new ways to look at the world. Often you will be frustrated because others may not accept your ideas without a completely logical explanation from you. Even then, they may not accept them. This type of stress is good, however, because it helps you grow intellectually. These situations enable you to see and understand things you never knew existed or give you new ways to look at things you see every day. The secret is to keep things in perspective and have a plan. Success requires understanding the things you want out of life *and* making a personal commitment to accomplish them. By staying focused on the important things in your life and efficiently applying all your resources—time, money, physical energy, and mental energy—you can achieve your goals and live a less stressful life.

You can still master a new computer game. You just have to do it in a way that does not interfere with attaining your long-run goals. You can have it all, but not all at the same time. If you plan your schedule sequentially, you do not have to refuse your roommate's challenge. You just need to schedule the game for a time when there are no pressing school deadlines.

ACTIVE LEARNING

Exercise 11.1 *On a separate sheet of paper, identify at least ten areas of bad stress in your life. Now list ten areas of good stress. Describe how you can control the negatively stressful areas of your life. Explain how stress can affect your health and academic performance.*

NUTRITION

Another key element in good personal health is eating right. Healthy eating enables your body to work at peak efficiency. Some experts believe that a diet composed of 40 percent carbohydrates, 30 percent proteins, and 30 percent fats is the best combination of foods. The American Cancer Society and other health groups encourage you to eat five servings a day of fruits and vegetables. It is often recommended that you eat four or five small meals rather than three large meals each day. Some believe that breakfast is the most important meal and will get you off to a fast start and keep your mind alert all day. This regimen will also help you keep your weight at a proper level and reduce your chance of illness.

Exercise 11.2 *On a separate sheet of paper, keep a record of what you eat for the next week. Do not forget snacks. Evaluate the nutritional balance and value of what you ate.*

Exercise 11.3 *Develop a menu for the coming week. Evaluate the nutritional balance and value of your menu.*

ACTIVE LEARNING

Exercise 11.4 *Plan a group dinner. Analyze how the meal meets the nutritional recommendations of the American Cancer Society.*

EXERCISE

Along with maintaining a good diet, it is important for you to keep your body in good physical shape so you can develop the stamina to meet the physical demands of school. It does not take much to maintain a reasonable level of fitness. You can accomplish this with just 20 to 30 minutes of exercise three or four times a week. You can build exercise into your day by walking to class, parking in distant parking lots, and using the stairs rather than the elevator. Some people enjoy team sports such as basketball, football, soccer, volleyball, and baseball. Others find individual exercise such as aerobics, running, weight lifting, swimming, and biking to be the best exercise for them. Still others enjoy sports they can do with one or two people, such as tennis, racquetball, squash, canoeing, or golf. The value of these activities goes well beyond the physical payoff; relief from stress and a sense of accomplishment usually accompany them. What you choose to do is far less important than the fact that you do *something*.

Exercise 11.5 *Get information about four places on your campus and in your community that offer opportunities for physical exercise. On a separate sheet of paper, list their names, locations, and telephone numbers, and write a brief description of the services and costs associated with each.*

Exercise 11.6 *On a separate sheet of paper, keep a record of how much and what kind of exercise you get during the next week. Explain why you chose each physical activity, and analyze how you can improve your performance. Discuss how exercise affects your health and academic performance.*

Exercise 11.7 *Participate in a walk-a-thon or some other exercise event of your choice. Write a brief paragraph describing how you benefited and what you learned from this activity.*

_____

_____

_____

_____

SLEEP

The subject of sleep comes last in this section because if you manage stress, eat right, and exercise regularly, you will naturally sleep better, wake up refreshed, and have enough energy to get you through the entire day. A good night's sleep starts with going to bed around the same time every night. To function effectively, most people need between seven and nine hours of sleep per night. If you stay up all night, you will not function very well the next day. Some students have studied all night for a big test only to fall asleep at sunrise and miss the whole exam. Even if they did make it to the exam, they typically did poorly since exhaustion kept them from thinking clearly.

Good sleeping habits start with a balanced lifestyle. If you develop a time schedule for a typical school week and study during daylight hours, you will not only get all your work done and have time for fun and exercise but will still get enough sleep to keep up the pace for the full semester. First-year students in particular do not get enough sleep. Many stay up until 2:00 or 3:00 every night during their first semester and find themselves exhausted after a few weeks of school.

Restful sleep comes from developing good sleep habits. Here are some suggestions to improve your sleep:

1. Avoid studying on your bed so your body will associate the bed only with sleep.

2. Try to make your room quiet and dark. If noisy roommates and neighbors make this difficult, use earplugs and block out the light.

3. Keep your room cool at night, between 65 and 68 degrees.

4. Go to bed and get up at the same time every day so your body gets used to a routine.

5. If you have trouble falling asleep, take a warm bath or shower before you go to bed. Try to eat just a light snack no less than two hours before bedtime.

6. Even though exercise helps you to sleep better, avoid exercising within four hours of bedtime since your body needs to unwind before going to sleep.

If you follow all these suggestions, you should sleep more soundly and wake up more refreshed. You will be rested enough to get to all of your classes and alert enough to pay close attention.

ACTIVE LEARNING

Exercise 11.8 *On a separate sheet of paper, keep a record for one week of how much sleep you get each night. Analyze how you can improve your sleep habits. Discuss how good sleep habits affect your health and academic performance.*

As you can see, good health can help you achieve your goals and will pay big dividends for the rest of your life. Stress management, good nutrition, practical exercise, and good sleep habits all contribute to your well-being and your attitude toward college and life.

▲ *Alcohol, Tobacco, and Drugs*

Alcohol, tobacco, and drugs are another set of choices you will confront. What you decide will tell you and others a great deal about who you are and what you stand for. Evidence of the harmful effects of these three substances is overwhelming, yet many people give in to them. Many young people think they are invincible and can handle these substances, but in reality they cannot.

If you understand who you are and know how to stand up for your values, you will find it easier to resist harmful substances. You will not have to conform to someone else's idea of what is right for you because you will be committed to your own well-being. When you make a personal commitment to your long-run success, you will have the courage to stick to it and to do what is right to get you where you want to go. Because you can think for yourself, you can look at the data and make a well-informed choice about alcohol, tobacco, and drugs. It is what a thinking person would do. Part of being well informed is knowing how these substances can impair the quality of life for those who abuse them.

Exercise 11.9 *Interview the person responsible for the alcohol, tobacco, and drug information office at your school. Identify the goals and objectives of this office and the services available. Write a short summary of what you found and how this service can be beneficial to you and others you know.*

_____

_____

_____

_____

_____

Exercise 11.10 *Interview a student who drinks alcohol heavily on weekends. Ask this student how, when, and why she or he drinks. Discuss what may be prompting the student to abuse alcohol. What part does peer pressure play in this person's choices? On a separate sheet of paper, write a paragraph describing your personal approach to the use of alcohol.*

Exercise 11.11 *In a short paragraph, define binge drinking. Compare your definition with those of classmates, and discuss the problems that arise from binge drinking.*

_____

_____

_____

_____

Exercise 11.12 *Research the laws associated with drug and alcohol use. Find out your college's policy on their use. Compare specific federal, state, and local laws with your college's policies on these issues.*

_____

_____

_____

_____

_____

Exercise 11.13 *Should colleges and universities have authority over student drug and alcohol use? On a separate sheet of paper, write an essay explaining your feelings on this issue.*

Exercise 11.14 *Make a list of facts that suggest you should be free to binge-drink. Make another list of facts that suggest you should* not *be free to binge-drink. Prepare a chart comparing the two arguments. What conclusions can you draw from this chart?*

▲ Sex and Sexually Transmitted Diseases

Another set of choices you will confront regards your involvement in sexual activities. You have to make your own choices about what is right for you, but just as with many other choices, your decision comes with personal responsibility and personal commitment. If your decision is to wait until you are married to have sexual relations, you are more likely to avoid contracting a sexually transmitted disease, and you will prevent an unplanned pregnancy and its effects on your future. As with alcohol, tobacco, and drug use, you should always use your thinking powers to evaluate the data before you make a decision that could have harmful or even deadly consequences.

Refraining from sex before marriage is usually the preferred choice, but the decision is yours, as well as the responsibility for the consequences of your actions. If you choose to engage in sexual relations, part of your personal responsibility is to take proper precautions to protect yourself and your partner from sexually transmitted diseases and unwanted pregnancy. You must make a personal commitment to follow these actions each time you engage in sex. Sex is a natural part of life, but there is a proper time and place for it. Remember, the choice is yours.

▲ Mental Health

Along with good physical health, you should strive to maintain good mental health. Good mental health means being able to cope with the normal trials and tribulations of everyday life. Most people have some "down days" and some "good days." It is important to realize that both kinds of days are normal and that life does bring some adversity. When you experience an adverse event, it is critical that you know how to bounce back. Unfortunately, not everyone can do this. Recognizing when things have gotten out of control and when to seek appropriate professional help is vital to your mental health.

Feeling anxious or sad when things change in your life is normal. Getting over it in a reasonable period is also normal. The death of a family member or a friend, the breakup of a marriage or other close relationship, or even bad grades can all be sources of anxiety or sadness. If you cannot shake your negative feelings after a reasonable period of time, you may need help.

The first step in reclaiming your mental health is being able to verbalize how you feel and why something bothers you. Talking often helps you understand exactly what is wrong. As you develop your personal journal throughout this course, your self-awareness will grow and putting your feelings in writing will get easier. A journal can help you self-diagnose your problems.

The next step is being able to talk to others about your problems. This should be someone you trust and whose advice you value, such as a parent, friend, religious leader, school counselor, or teacher. There is no need to suffer alone if you use the numerous sources of help available. You will probably respond well to outside help. You have many great things to accomplish in your life, and good mental health is critical to achieving them.

As you learn to recognize and cope with problems in your own life, you will be able to perceive when others need help. For example, a friend may be depressed over the loss of a loved one and be unable to deal with it after a reasonable period of time. Friends help friends with their problems.

Maintaining a healthy balance in your life, both physically and mentally, is a vital part of a successful life. Truly successful people balance all the conflicting demands on their time and energy and learn to cope with the crises that come their way. You will have a successful career, a good family life, a healthy lifestyle, many friends, and a satisfying involvement in your community and your religion when you have a clear view of what is important to you and commit yourself to accomplishing your goals. When you approach life this way, you will find that you spend time on the important things and reduce the stress in your life.

Once you have established your priorities, the basic principles of managing stress, eating right, exercising regularly, and getting enough sleep will only enhance your life. Treating your body with respect and not abusing it with alcohol, tobacco, drugs, or irresponsible sex will greatly increase your chances of success. As you learn to maintain good physical health and make wise decisions, you will be better able to maintain good mental health by keeping things in perspective and knowing when you need to seek help.

CHAPTER HIGHLIGHTS

1. If you apply the principles of personal responsibility and commitment, and maintain good physical and mental health, you will increase your chances to succeed.

2. Because of your strong sense of self-awareness, you can see the value of keeping yourself in good physical and mental shape.

3. When you are in good physical and mental condition, you have the stamina to keep working toward your life goals.

4. Developing a set of personal values is a byproduct of a college education.

5. A firm grasp of who you are and what you want to be reduces the stress in your life. You know who you are and do not let others define what is right for you.

6. Other elements that lower stress are good nutrition, regular exercise, and adequate sleep.

7. Part of formulating your set of personal values is deciding how you will deal with alcohol, drugs, tobacco, and sex.

8. Good health involves both physical and mental health. Learn to understand yourself and your moods. Recognize when you need to get help.

CHAPTER HIGHLIGHTS

CASE STUDY

Salina's Sleepy Summer

The summer afternoon sun shone brightly on Salina's face and soon brought her out of a deep sleep. As she sat up, she looked at her clock radio and realized she had been asleep for more than two hours. She had planned to just grab a short nap after lunch and then head off to her 2:00 English class. At first, Salina thought missing English was not a big deal since nothing very interesting ever happened there anyway. Yet it did bother her that this was the second class this week she had missed. She just could not keep her eyes open in the afternoons. Salina thought, "It must be this hot summer weather that is making me so sleepy. Yeah. I think that must be it, plus I'm stuck with the most boring professor in the world for my 8:00 biology lecture every morning. Who would have guessed I would get the only professor who actually takes attendance and lowers your grade if you are not there?"

Salina enrolled for the summer term to get a head start on college. She had heard that the courses were easier in the summer. She did not realize that classes met every day and that class attendance would affect her grade. Most mornings she barely made it into her seat before the attendance sheet reached her. By the time the 75-minute class was over, the cafeteria was closed, so she used the vending machines for breakfast. She rationalized that since cream-filled cupcakes contained wheat, eggs, milk, and other healthy ingredients, they made a nutritious breakfast. Cupcakes would have to do until the lunch line opened at 11:00 A.M. One good thing about college is that you finally got to eat what you want and as much as you want. Salina really had developed a taste for the university's own brand of ice cream. Some days ice cream was all she had for lunch.

Somehow college seemed to be sapping all of Salina's energy and time. Although she always started her homework at 7:00 each night, it was often after 2:00 A.M. before she got to bed. The biggest problem was all the drop-by visitors. Jeremy, her biology lab partner, was the exception. He was a junior who was also taking biology in the summer because he heard it was easier. He invited Salina to his apartment several times for parties with his roommates. Salina had been popular in high school but had never been much of a drinker. No matter how much she tried, she just could not keep up with Jeremy and his friends when it came to drinking. Sometimes she barely remembered how she made it back to her dorm room. She usually felt so wiped out after one of Jeremy's parties that she got nothing done the next day.

While she really enjoyed all the fun parts of college, deep down she felt things were out of control. She was not doing well in her courses, and she was always tired and stressed out. Her grade in biology was already going to be one grade lower because of all the classes she had missed. As she sat on the side of her bed, she began to think about the things she missed most. In the first three weeks of school, she had made some new friends, but they were not like the people at home. What she missed most was home-cooked meals and the long bike rides that always helped her calm down. She had not ridden her bike since the first day of class.

Salina decided she needed to splash some cold water on her face to wake up fully. In the dorm bathroom, she met her floor's resident assistant (RA). When the RA saw Salina's face, she knew something was wrong. When she asked Salina how she was doing, Salina blurted out all her troubles and told her everything that was on her mind.

If you were the RA, what would you advise Salina to do to get her life and health in order?

Personal Journal

CRITICAL THINKING

Personal Journal 11.1 Select three topics discussed in this chapter and describe how you feel about them. How have your opinions changed since you came to college? Compare your feelings today with how you felt about these topics four years ago. How do you think you may feel about these issues four years from now? What changes do you think you need to make in your lifestyle? What will it take for you to make these changes?

_____

_____

_____

_____

_____

_____

_____

_____

DIVERSITY

Personal Journal 11.2 "Everyone's choices about health, smoking, alcohol, drugs, sex, and numerous other issues are no one else's business and should not be part of a college course or textbook." Do you agree or disagree? Explain your answer.

_____

_____

_____

_____

_____

_____

_____

_____

_____

CHAPTER QUIZ

n_search

1. Why is knowing who you are a prerequisite to establishing a set of personal values?

_____

_____

_____

_____

_____

2. What is meant by the phrase "a balanced life is a successful life"?

_____

_____

_____

_____

_____

3. Is all stress in your life bad? Explain your answer.

_____

_____

_____

_____

_____

4. Why do issues of alcohol, tobacco, drugs, and sex involve personal responsibility and personal commitment?

_____

_____

_____

_____

_____

5. What role does self-awareness play in helping you develop your own set of personal values?

_____

_____

_____

_____

_____

CHAPTER 12

Campus Money Management

CHAPTER OBJECTIVES

After reading this chapter, you will understand why:

- Money is one of the important means used to accomplish your life goals.
- Money allows you choices in your life, but you must accept personal responsibility for your choices.
- Successful money management means aligning your spending with your life goals.
- Budgeting gives you control of your money and makes it easier to reach your life goals.
- Sticking with your budget is easier if you understand how effective money management helps you accomplish your life goals.

After reading this chapter, you will know how to:

- Align your life goals and your spending habits.
- Use a budget to control your use of money.
- Make a school-year and a monthly budget.
- Use debt wisely.

Money is a necessary ingredient in everyone's life. It gives us the means to achieve many of our life goals. Unfortunately, some people use money to measure their success and happiness. Money, like education, allows us to have choices in our lives. For example, if all you have is $4 to spend for lunch, the choice of where to eat is more limited than if you have $100. However, having choices means you must accept personal responsibility for the decisions you make. Just as you have taken personal responsibility for other aspects of your life as a college student, you must assume responsibility for your financial affairs. Fortunately, money management is easy once you grasp the basic principles and take time to plan.

▲ Aligning Your Life Goals and Your Spending

The key to successful money management is to align your spending with your life goals. You may have planned to be in college for many years. A vital part of that plan was ensuring you had saved enough money. You and your family may have had to limit your spending so you could afford to go to college. Perhaps you gave up things such as vacations and a new car so you could accomplish a bigger, longer-run goal: a college education. Money management is like a NASCAR driver who calculates how much fuel is needed to finish a 500-mile race and then makes sure the pit crew has enough on hand before the race starts. It would be a sad loss if the driver led the entire race and ran out of fuel on the last lap. More careful planning could have prevented that loss. Similarly, when you plan for college, be sure you have enough "fuel" on hand to finish the "race."

RITA ROSE
1543 OAK LANE
SPRINGVALE, CA 91264

233

20

PAY TO THE
ORDER OF

DOLLARS

STATE BANK

FOR

Perhaps the most important ingredient of good money management is a realistic budget. The word *budget* often connotes doing without things and not having any fun. Budgeting, however, allows you to control your money so you can do both the really important things and the fun things. With a budget, you are less likely to face unexpected financial surprises that can prevent you from achieving your goals. Budgeting is about choices and anticipating difficulties before they arise so you have time to make adjustments. For example, if you make up a budget in July for the upcoming school year, you will discover right away whether you will have enough money to pay spring semester fees, and still have money to live on. Since you know this in July, you can start looking for a fall job to earn enough money for the spring. This is a much better choice than finding yourself broke on the first day of spring semester.

Good budgeting also means that if you spend a little less each week of the fall semester, you will be able to afford an indulgence, such as a ski trip, for a few days during Christmas break. In this case, you get to have fun because you have budgeted for it. Developing a budget is easy; the hard part is sticking to it. You will find it easier to live within your budget when you realize the benefits.

DEVELOPING YOUR BUDGET

Most students find they need two budgets. The first is a school-year budget that includes the dates when tuition and fees are due. The second is a monthly budget in which you plan for your everyday income and living expenses.

The School-Year Budget Before the start of each school year, you will need to find out when the "big money days" are—when things like tuition and room and board are due and how much you will need to pay for them. For schools on a semester system, the "big money days" normally come in mid-August and mid-December. Most schools announce their fees for the next school year in late April. Students need to file their financial aid and loan applications before the end of April. By the end of May, you should have enough information on costs and financial aid to begin developing next year's school budget. A typical budget will look something like Figure 12.1 (see page 206).

The school-year budget starts with school fees, the biggest and most uncontrollable items. In the example in Figure 12.1, these fees are projected to be $5,000 per semester, with an additional $300 for books. The day-to-day living expenses for things like movies, entertainment, and laundry are estimated at $120 per month, or approximately $30 per week. Since these expenses will be ongoing whether you are in school or at home, they are included as 26-week expenses (18 weeks at school and 8 weeks at home) for each semester. The cost of college for this budget is $6,080 per semester.

The second half of Figure 12.1 shows how you will meet these expenses. You have $1,250 per semester in financial aid, and your good grades have earned you a scholarship of $500 per semester. This reduces the cost of a semester of school to $4,330. If you save $2,000 from your summer job and use $5,400 from your college savings, you will need to earn $630 each semester to meet your college

FIGURE 12.1 The School-Year Budget

	Fall Semester	Spring Semester
School expenses		
Tuition	$2,500	$2,500
Room and board	2,400	2,400
Fees	100	100
Total	$5,000	$5,000
Living expenses		
($30/week for 26 weeks)	780	780
Books	300	300
Total	$6,080	$6,080
Less		
1. Financial aid	$1,250	$1,250
2. Scholarship	500	500
3. Summer job earnings	1,000	1,000
4. College savings	2,700	2,700
5. School-year job earnings	630	630
Total	$6,080	$6,080

expenses. You will need to work about eight hours per week to earn this amount ($5.50/hour × 8 hours/week × 15 weeks/semester = $660 before taxes).

Now you have a financial plan that shows you how you will meet your college expenses during the coming school year. You know how much money you need and how you will obtain it. If things do not work out, you can quickly adjust for changes such as a decrease in financial aid or the loss of a scholarship. You know you need to save $2,000 from your summer job and work eight hours a week to cover your living expenses. With this plan in place, you can concentrate on your schoolwork rather than wasting time worrying about money.

ACTIVE LEARNING

Exercise 12.1 *Using the blank form in Figure 12.2 on page 207, develop a school-year budget for the next semester.*

FIGURE 12.2 Your School-Year Budget

	Fall Semester	Spring Semester
School expenses		
Tuition	_____	_____
Room and board	_____	_____
Fees	_____	_____
Total	_____	_____
Living expenses		
($30/week for 26 weeks)	_____	_____
Books	_____	_____
Other	_____	_____
Total	_____	_____
Less		
1. Financial aid	_____	_____
2. Scholarship	_____	_____
3. Summer job earnings	_____	_____
4. College savings	_____	_____
5. School-year job earnings	_____	_____
Total	_____	_____

The Monthly Budget The next step in the budgeting process is to see if you have enough money during the summer months, beginning immediately at the end of the spring semester in mid-May (see Figure 12.3 on pages 208–209). You keep a running total of your cash situation in the same way you would keep your checkbook.

Your budget starts with an initial balance of zero on May 1. To this you add the money you expect to receive during May to get a value for total cash available. In this case, you anticipate a May take-home pay of $350 from your summer job, making your available cash $350. Living expenses of $120 for the month of May are subtracted from the total cash available, leaving a net cash balance of $230. This amount is carried forward as the opening balance for the month of June. Your summer job nets you $650 in June, giving you $880. Since your living expenses for June are $120, you end that month with $760. Repeat the process for July.

FIGURE 12.3 **The Monthly Budget**

	May	June	July	August	September	October
1. Balance forward	0	230	760	1,290	745	775
INCOME						
2. Summer job	350	650	650	350		
3. School job				75	150	150
4. Savings				2,700		
5. Financial aid				1,250		
6. Scholarship				500		
7. Total cash available (sum 1–6)	350	880	1410	6,165	895	925
EXPENSES						
8. School fees				5,000		
9. Books				300		
10. Living expenses	120	120	120	120	120	120
11. Total expenses (sum 8–10)	120	120	120	5,420	120	120
12. Ending balance (7 less 11)	230	760	1290	745	775	805

In August, you start the month with $1,290. Assuming you will work only two weeks in August on your summer job, add $350 to that amount. Then add $75 for your new job at school. You will need $2,700 from your college savings and $1,750 of financial aid and scholarship money to meet your school fees of $5,000, book expenses of $300, and living expenses of $120 that are due during August. After paying all your bills, you should have $745 left in your account. Continue this process for each month of the coming school year.

As you carry out this procedure, you may discover you do not have enough money for fees, books, and living expenses for the spring semester. You need to earn an extra $135 during December. This might come from working part-time over the holiday break. You need this money for books and living expenses

	November	December	January	February	March	April
1. Balance forward	805	835	375	30	60	90
INCOME						
2. Summer job		135				
3. School job	150	75	75	150	150	150
4. Savings		2,700				
5. Financial aid		1,250				
6. Scholarship		500				
7. Total cash available (sum 1–6)	955	5,495	450	180	210	240
EXPENSES						
8. School fees		5,000				
9. Books			300			
10. Living expenses	120	120	120	120	120	120
11. Total expenses (sum 8–10)	120	5,120	420	120	120	120
12. Ending balance (7 less 11)	835	375	30	60	90	120

for January and February, and to give you a small surplus for unexpected expenses during January. You might ask your summer employer if he or she needs help over the holidays, or you can look for employment when you are home for Thanksgiving.

Budgeting puts you in control of your finances and makes it easier to reach your life goals. It also reduces your stress about money. The process of budgeting makes you think about your future and recognize the trade-offs you need to make.

ACTIVE LEARNING

Exercise 12.2 *Using the blank form in Figure 12.4 on pages 210–211, develop a monthly budget for the next year.*

FIGURE 12.4 **Your Monthly Budget**

	May	June	July	August	September	October
1. Balance forward						
INCOME						
2. Summer job						
3. School job						
4. Savings						
5. Financial aid						
6. Scholarship						
7. Total cash available (sum 1–6)						
EXPENSES						
8. School fees						
9. Books						
10. Living expenses						
11. Total expenses (sum 8–10)						
12. Ending balance (7 less 11)						

ACTIVE LEARNING

Exercise 12.3 *In your personal budget, you have a category for "other" expenses. On a separate sheet of paper, identify and rank a list of 20 possible "other" expenses.*

ACTIVE LEARNING

Exercise 12.4 *A summer job offers you a way to earn money to cover expenses for the coming semester. On a separate sheet of paper, construct a list of twelve potential summer jobs. For each job, list possible locations, potential earnings, and anticipated expenses associated with accepting that job (housing, meals, transportation, clothing). Describe how each job supports your academic interests. Then rank the jobs according to how each would best meet your situation.*

	November	December	January	February	March	April
1. Balance forward						
INCOME						
2. Summer job						
3. School job						
4. Savings						
5. Financial aid						
6. Scholarship						
7. Total cash available (sum 1–6)						
EXPENSES						
8. School fees						
9. Books						
10. Living expenses						
11. Total expenses (sum 8–10)						
12. Ending balance (7 less 11)						

▲ Credit Cards, ATM Cards, and Debit Cards

One of the biggest hazards you face in college is debt. It seems that every day your mailbox is filled with offers for fantastic credit opportunities. Be careful! Credit cards can sometimes help you manage your money and allow you to accomplish things, but if you use them carelessly, they will get you into trouble very quickly. Most student budgets have little room for extras, especially if they are paid for with a credit card (see Figure 12.5 on page 213). Keep your credit card charges as low as possible. They should not exceed your ability to

pay them off each month. Balances carried beyond a month impose interest rates as high as 18 to 22 percent per year. Typically, if you make just the minimum payment each month, you will pay off little of the debt. Even a small charge can take months or sometimes years to pay off.

A common question is: How much debt is too much? When it comes to credit cards, if you cannot pay off the balance when the bill comes, it is too much debt. Experts say you have too much debt if your monthly debt payments take 20 percent or more of your monthly income. The recommended level is 10 percent or less. Monthly debt payments include things such as car payments, credit card bills, student loan payments, and so on.

ATMs (automatic teller machines) have made getting cash a simple matter, whatever the day or time. Like everything else, they can make your life easier when used wisely. The best plan is to pay yourself each week with a regular ATM withdrawal. This is the cash you will use to meet day-to-day expenses. Your goal should be to make this money last until your next payday. This system keeps your daily spending in check and helps you keep withdrawal fees, if any, to a minimum. Be sure to save your receipts and record your withdrawals in your checkbook as soon as possible. One simple way to monitor your spending is to write down how you spent the money on the back of your ATM receipt.

Another way to control your spending is to use a debit card, which deducts the amount of your purchase directly from your bank account. Similar to an electronic check, a debit card can be used just like cash, thus avoiding a large credit card bill at the end of the month.

Controlling your money is an important part of controlling your life. It is a key ingredient in successfully reaching your life goals. Students who have made a personal commitment to their success and taken personal responsibility for their decisions recognize that they must also assume responsibility for their financial affairs. To take control of your finances is to understand how to budget and to efficiently use your money to accomplish your life goals.

FIGURE 12.5 Average Spending by Young Adults in a Year (average age, 21)

Item	Males	Females
Food, including eating out	$1,915	$1,903
Rent	2,276	2,226
Utilities	686	716
Clothing	664	1,233
Transportation (car payments, maintenance, insurance, public transit)	3,045	1,701
Health care	200	253
Entertainment	1,144	698
Personal care	140	297
Education (tuition, books, fees)	1,592	1,351
Reading material	64	60
Taxes (all levels)	725	401
Miscellaneous	404	388

Source: *Consumer Expenditure Survey, 1996–97,* U.S. Bureau of Labor Statistics.

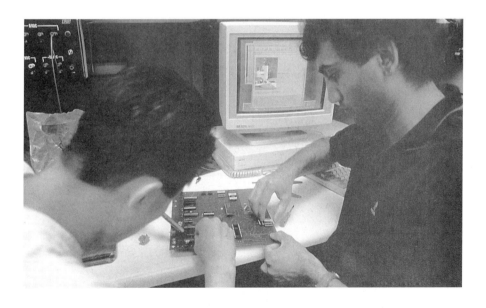

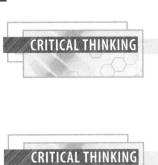

Exercise 12.5 *During a one-month period, count the number of credit card offers you receive. Analyze the offers by fees, interest rates, promotions, and amount of credit offered. Why do you think credit card companies are so interested in giving credit cards to college students who are basically unemployed?*

Exercise 12.6 *On a separate sheet of paper, write a plan for investigating a financial aid package to support your education. Examine the availability and dollar value of loans, scholarships, grants, and work-study opportunities.*

Exercise 12.7 *On a separate sheet of paper, analyze the differences among work-study, employment, and volunteer opportunities on your campus. Explain the costs and benefits related to each opportunity.*

Exercise 12.8 *Write a brief comparison of the costs and benefits of living in a dormitory, at home, or in an off-campus apartment.*

_____

_____

_____

_____

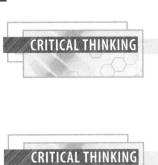

Exercise 12.9 *Visit the financial aid office at your school and determine the types of services it provides. Write a description of the options available to you.*

_____

_____

_____

_____

ACTIVE LEARNING

Exercise 12.10 *Visit at least two banks and one credit union located at or near your school. Write down the types of services they offer and the fees and promotions associated with these services. Describe the differences between a bank and a credit union. Determine which financial institution offers you the better deal. Explain what factors made you choose this institution.*

CRITICAL THINKING

Exercise 12.11 *On a separate sheet of paper, compare the benefits and costs to you of an ATM card, a credit card, and a debit card.*

CRITICAL THINKING

Exercise 12.12 *Your roommate has considerably more money to spend than you do and is always inviting you to do things that you cannot afford. Describe three ways you can continue to be friends despite your different financial resources.*

_____

_____

_____

_____

ACTIVE LEARNING

Exercise 12.13 *On a separate sheet of paper, construct a time plan showing how and when you could earn extra money at a part-time job.*

COLLABORATIVE LEARNING

Exercise 12.14 *Break up into groups of three or four and brainstorm about the free activities and programs available at your college or in the community. Then share your findings with the other groups to generate a large list of free programs and activities.*

_____

_____

_____

_____

ACTIVE LEARNING

Exercise 12.15 *Identify ten web sites that offer cost savings on travel, books, and other items.*

_____

_____

_____

_____

_____

CHAPTER HIGHLIGHTS

1. Money is a necessary ingredient in your ability to achieve your life goals.

2. As a college student, you should assume personal responsibility for your financial affairs.

3. Successful money management begins with aligning your spending with your life goals.

4. Budgeting is a valuable tool in your financial planning.

5. Budgeting gives you control over your spending so that your life is more fulfilled.

6. The combination of a school-year budget and a monthly budget can give you the information you need to use your money wisely.

7. When you create a budget, you know how you will pay for expenses before the semester starts. This will reduce your money worries and allow you to concentrate on your schoolwork.

CHAPTER HIGHLIGHTS

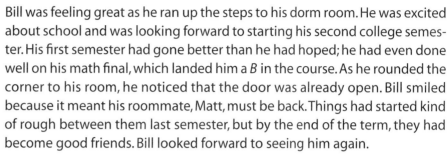

Matt's Money Management Monster

Bill was feeling great as he ran up the steps to his dorm room. He was excited about school and was looking forward to starting his second college semester. His first semester had gone better than he had hoped; he had even done well on his math final, which landed him a *B* in the course. As he rounded the corner to his room, he noticed that the door was already open. Bill smiled because it meant his roommate, Matt, must be back. Things had started kind of rough between them last semester, but by the end of the term, they had become good friends. Bill looked forward to seeing him again.

Bill bounded into the room and threw his bags on his bed. "Matt! Good to see you again!" said Bill. Right away, Matt told Bill all about his ski trip during break. Although the trip was a last-minute idea, Matt had a great time with his old friends from high school. Bill said that it was so much better than working at the drugstore for the entire break as he had to do.

Matt and Bill had both made good grades their first semester. Matt had earned just over a 3.0 average for the semester. His parents were pleased, and some of his friends at home said they were shocked at how well he had done. Matt attributed his success to a good high school, good time management, and not having to work while in school.

Despite all the excitement, Bill noticed some tension in Matt's voice. Then Bill realized that Matt was sitting at his desk, looking at his checkbook and a pile of mail that had accumulated over the semester break. Bill knew "that look." It was the same one his father had when he was paying bills. Bill finally got up enough courage to ask Matt what was bothering him. Matt admitted that his father had put a great deal of trust in him and given Matt all his college money in the fall to manage the entire year. Matt's father simply warned him, "When it's gone, it's gone."

Matt's mother had gone back to work when Matt started high school and saved all her income for his college expenses. Like everyone else, Matt had paid his tuition, room and board, and fees last month, and he thought he had enough money to last to the end of the school year.

Matt's major financial problem was that he had accepted several credit card offers he had received last semester and used them for his ski trip and for Christmas presents. The mail on his desk was made up of these credit card bills. Even if he used all the money he had for the rest of the semester, he still could not pay all of them off. "The funny part," Matt said, "was that I didn't go crazy and spend lots of money at any one time. Somehow $20 here and $50 there sure added up. I can't believe I spent $1,865.39! Now everyone wants their money. How am I going to pay all these bills? My father is going to be really disappointed in me." Matt looked anxiously at Bill and asked, "What do you think I should do?"

If you were Bill, what advice would you give Matt?

Personal Journal

CRITICAL THINKING

Personal Journal 12.1 Describe an experience when you succeeded because of good financial planning. How do you feel about this experience?

_____

_____

_____

_____

_____

_____

_____

_____

CRITICAL THINKING

Personal Journal 12.2 Describe an experience when you wanted to accomplish something but failed because you did not think about the financial aspects beforehand. How do you feel about this experience? What would you do differently now if you had a chance to do it all over?

_____

_____

_____

_____

_____

_____

_____

CRITICAL THINKING

Personal Journal 12.3 List at least five things you learned from the previous two experiences that will help you plan the financial part of your college education.

_____

_____

_____

_____

_____

_____

_____

_____

DIVERSITY

Personal Journal 12.4 What are the differences, if any, between the way women and men spend their money? Do they budget their money differently? Explain your answers.

_____

_____

_____

_____

_____

_____

_____

_____

_____

_____

CHAPTER QUIZ

1. Why is taking personal responsibility for your financial affairs consistent with making a personal commitment to your college education?

_____

_____

_____

_____

_____

2. What are the advantages of budgeting while you are in college?

_____

_____

_____

_____

_____

3. Explain the role of a school-year budget and a monthly budget in your overall college financial planning.

_____

_____

_____

_____

CHAPTER 13

Beyond Diversity: Understanding, Tolerance, and Respect

CHAPTER OBJECTIVES

After reading this chapter, you will understand why:

- Diversity is an integral part of your world.
- Laws, customs, and expectations affect your behavior.
- There are differences between tolerance and respect.
- Diversity, understanding, tolerance, and respect should be included in the college curriculum.

After reading this chapter, you will know how to:

- Examine your personal attitudes about diversity, tolerance, and respect.
- Make a personal commitment to respect other cultures.
- Reflect about how you can eliminate bias and accept others.
- Maximize your personal growth in valuing diversity.
- Recognize diversity, understanding, tolerance, and respect in your college curriculum and in your community.

On October 12, 1999, demographers estimated the world's population at 6 billion. They also estimated that every second, five people are born and two die, for a net gain to the population of three people. If you were born in 1982, when the world's population was about 4.5 billion, the growth in the global population to 6 billion represents a 34 percent increase in 17 years. If you were born in 1949, when the world's population was about 2.5 billion, the 1999 figure represents an increase of 146 percent. The projections call for the earth's population to increase to 8 billion before leveling off in the middle of the 21st century.

All these additional people live in the same amount of physical space, which suggests that the earth's population is challenged to make careful choices about resources, including land, water, and all other natural resources. If the overall goal of the people of the world is to live in peace and harmony amid diminishing resources, individuals, communities, and nations must work together. World problems suggest that all people are not working together for peace and harmony. Clearly, world conflicts spawn a host of unanswered questions that puzzle all humans about the quality and future of life for all of the earth's inhabitants.

The United States of America is known as the "great melting pot" because during the past 200 years, countless individuals have sought and found religious and political freedom here, where the ideals of freedom and individual differences are welcome. Contemporary America continues to welcome all people to live and work in the United States. The diverse nature of America is viewed as a remarkable grand experiment. Many countries around the world respect, admire, and seek to duplicate America's accomplishment. The United States embraces the richness of diverse cultures, customs, and traditions as integral to the American heritage.

▲ Understanding Others in Your College Community

College may be giving you your first opportunity to be a part of a diversified community with people of many cultures, traditions, religions, countries, and

continents. This is an extraordinary opportunity for you. The rights and responsibilities associated with being a part of this global community will test your ability to be open-minded, wholehearted, and appreciative of differences. If this is a new experience for you, you may feel uncomfortable at first. Your experience can be frustrating or exciting depending on how you respond to it. You can choose to appreciate and recognize differences, or you can choose to ignore them.

As a college student, you may find yourself in a community where, for the first time, you study and discuss issues and conflicts in a world context rather than local ones. Because of the variety of people in your classrooms and dormitory, you may for the first time befriend someone from another country. The fundamental differences you notice in the person's clothing, food, customs, and language may be striking, but the similarities will be quite obvious too. You both have chosen the same college, live in the same dormitory, attend the same classes, may like the same restaurants, or read the same books. Perhaps you attend the same sporting events and go to the same concerts. Scientists report that less than one-tenth of 1 percent of human genetics accounts for any biological differences between races and genders. To put it simply, human beings are more alike than they are different.

Though the biological differences are minuscule, our cultural differences may be large. Many cultural differences reflect the socialization patterns of our background that were imposed on us by our cultures, religions, politics, and families. These differences are not necessarily problems. Instead, you should view them as opportunities to enrich your life. The rich insights you can gain from understanding the differences in the way people view such issues as politics, religion, and music should be your personal quest as you become an educated person. College provides you with the invaluable opportunity to develop a scholarly knowledge of the diverse world, as well as a personal understanding of diversity through your interactions with other people. You may be required to study diversity in your history or literature classes, but you will truly comprehend diversity as you interact daily with other students and faculty members. A virtual journey around the world begins with the opportunities you have to know people from many diverse backgrounds.

Recognizing and appreciating diversity as part of the teaching and learning process also strengthens your ability to develop your personal values. By making your learning more relevant to your life, you may change your attitudes and beliefs, or you may strengthen your old values. It is up to you to learn and grow from your experiences.

Exercise 13.1 *Interview some family members and trace your family genealogy for at least three generations. On a separate sheet of paper, list the number of countries represented in your background. What customs or traditions from those countries have stayed with your family through the years?*

Exercise 13.2 *Interview ten students and identify what countries are represented in at least two generations of their families.*

Exercise 13.3 *Attend a religious service that is unfamiliar to your religious tradition. On a separate sheet of paper, write a short essay describing what you learned and how it differs from tradition in your own religion.*

Exercise 13.4 *Describe three events or conversations in which you experienced a high regard for something someone else said or did. How did that change your feelings about each person?*

▲ Laws and Customs

Laws outline a set of defined expectations imposed on a group by a governing body to inform its citizens about how to behave. Some laws are more equitable than others. Each country determines its laws through its own form of government. The laws of the United States reflect the mandates of its citizens at the local, state, and national levels. At your college or university, you cannot ignore these laws, and you will have to follow additional policies set up within the framework of your school. Following are some specific federal civil rights laws that influence your college's policies and ultimately affect you.

The **Civil Rights Act of 1964** protects an individual's constitutional rights in public facilities and public education, and prohibits discrimination in federally assisted programs. In 1972, **Title IX of the Education Amendments** prohibited sex discrimination, including sexual harassment. The act was amended by the **Civil Rights Act of 1991**, which provided for the elimination of discrimination in the private and federal workplace on the basis of sex, race, religion, and national origin.

The **Office of Civil Rights (OCR)** of the U.S. Department of Education protects students from harassment and violence based on race, color, national origin, sex, and disability. Additional state and local laws further define and expand this federal law. Fundamentally, these laws seek to eliminate sexual harassment and hate crimes. At the same time, these laws are intended to recognize the First Amendment rights of students and employees.

In May 1999, a Supreme Court decision further opened the doors for teachers, administrators, and school boards to be sued for allowing or deliberately ignoring incidences of sexual harassment among peers.[1] This decision stated that educators could be held accountable for financial damages related to known acts of sexual harassment between peers. In fact, there were no damage limits in this Title IX litigation that furthered the protection of both male and female students from unlawful sexual harassment in all school programs.[2] Title IX specifically states that a student should feel safe and comfortable walking down the halls of his or her school. School is a place for learning and growing, and sexual harassment hinders that process.

Title VII of the Civil Rights Act of 1964 defines the limits of discriminatory practices related to personnel actions affecting employees or applicants for employment. The **Equal Employment Opportunity Commission (EEOC)** regulates the enforcement of and has power over the issuance of these rules.[3]

Title II of the Americans with Disabilities Act of 1990 prohibits discrimination by public entities on the basis of an individual's disability. The OCR ensures equal access to education and promoting educational excellence in the United States. **Section 504 of the Rehabilitation Act of 1973** first prohibited discrimination by disability. The **Age Discrimination Act of 1975** then prohibited age discrimination. These acts reflect a national commitment to eliminate discrimination in work and school.

▲ Customs, Traditions, Respect, and Tolerance

Customs are habitual courses of action or commonly practiced or observed actions. There are customs that are unique for families, cities, countries, or entire cultures. A remarkable variety of customs exists among the world's different societies. Yet most customs are outside formal law. For example, in a few countries it is customary for women to marry by age 14, whereas in the United States it is the exception. For many years, it was a Catholic custom to eat fish on Friday. Today eating fish on Fridays is not the custom for most Catholics in the United States.

---

1. *Davis v. Monroe County Board of Education.*
2. http://www.ed.gov/offices/OCR/ocrshpam.html.
3. http://www.dol.gov/dol/oasam/public/regs/statutes/2000e-16.htm.

Traditions relate to the handing down of beliefs or customs by word of mouth or by example without written instructions. For example, naming the first son in a family after the father, grandfather, and great-grandfather is an unwritten tradition in some families. It is passed down from one generation to the next, implying that merit and honor are associated with the tradition.

Respect means to consider someone deserving of high regard. Your high regard for the work of a great carpenter reflects your respect for his attention to detail and the quality of his work. You might respect a friend for something she has done such as competing successfully in an athletic event or a scholarly activity. The high regard relates to what you value and how the outcome of a particular action impresses you.

Tolerance is sympathy or indulgence for beliefs or practices differing from one's own. For example, some college cafeterias offer vegetarian meals in addition to their regular menu.

Tolerance and *respect* both connote a willingness to accept differences. However, respect goes beyond simply enduring differences; rather, it suggests appreciation, indicating that you value different cultures, customs, races, genders, physical limitations, and individual preferences.

Definitions of *diversity* are found in public laws and many fundamental value statements. The civil rights laws incorporate the ideas of diversity in affirmative action legislation and all civil rights legislation, but diversity permeates our daily lives as we live in harmony with the different traditions and customs of our neighbors near and far.

Graham Spanier, president of Penn State University, describes three ideas that are central to promoting diversity in a college setting:[4]

1. Expose students to a variety of cultural and international perspectives to prepare them for the future.

2. Foster a humane society where everyone feels welcome by eliminating disrespect and harassment while working toward civility and acceptance of all individuals.

3. Promote the development of character, conscience, citizenship, respect for others, and social responsibility.

These expectations of all students, faculty, and staff are conducive to establishing a climate of diversity and civility. When specific expectations are established for individuals, especially in a learning environment, results can be dramatic. Clearly articulating the expectations of any group, society, or person helps individuals make more informed choices and value diversity.

Legislation alone cannot dictate acceptance and tolerance of diversity. A personal commitment to being open-minded, wholehearted, and responsible leads individuals to adopt civility and respect for and tolerance of all differences. Tolerance can lead to respecting and valuing others in a diverse society.

---

4. Spanier, Graham, *A Framework to Foster Diversity at Penn State: 1998–2003*, Feb. 1998, page 1.

ACTIVE LEARNING

Exercise 13.5 *On a separate sheet of paper, write an essay describing how civil rights legislation relates to the ideas of respect and tolerance.*

COLLABORATIVE LEARNING

Exercise 13.6 *In groups of four or five students, discuss the meaning of* respect *as described in this chapter. Write three brief statements summarizing the major points that your group makes.*

_____

_____

_____

_____

_____

ACTIVE LEARNING

Exercise 13.7 *Suppose you belong to a club that is related to your major. During regularly scheduled meetings, one member repeatedly harasses another student sexually. Describe how you would deal with the situation.*

_____

_____

_____

_____

_____

CRITICAL THINKING

Exercise 13.8 *One of your classmates is from a foreign country and does not speak English very well. Identify three things you can do to make that student more comfortable in your classroom.*

_____

_____

_____

_____

_____

ACTIVE LEARNING

Exercise 13.9 *Your roommate's favorite fragrance is offensive to you. In a short paragraph, describe how you might handle the situation with understanding and respect.*

_____

_____

_____

_____

_____

COLLABORATIVE LEARNING

Exercise 13.10 *One of your classmates is profiled in the school paper for her outstanding contribution in a varsity soccer match. Pair up with another classmate and discuss how the class might acknowledge her accomplishment.*

COLLABORATIVE LEARNING

Exercise 13.11 *The class divides into two groups that will debate the following issue: "Did Title IX change higher education for the better?" Explain your group's position in this debate.*

_____

_____

_____

_____

_____

CRITICAL THINKING

Exercise 13.12 *On a separate sheet of paper, describe in one paragraph the qualities you expect of a good friend. Describe in another paragraph the qualities you expect of a classmate. Compare and contrast these expectations.*

COLLABORATIVE LEARNING

Exercise 13.13 *A Native American student comes from a reservation where casino gambling produces vast amounts of revenue for the reservation. During class, another student expresses strong beliefs against gambling. Discuss as a class whether these students can be friends. If so, how might they go about overcoming their differences?*

COLLABORATIVE LEARNING

Exercise 13.14 *You and several friends are enrolled in a class where the professor routinely makes unkind, rude, and seemingly unfair remarks to your group. Identify how you and your friends can resolve your conflict with this professor. List six strategies the group should consider, and discuss them in class.*

_____

_____

_____

_____

_____

_____

CHAPTER HIGHLIGHTS

1. Diversity is a valuable component of any community, including your college community.

2. Laws and customs dictate your behaviors; however, your own beliefs and personal values influence your behavior.

3. People can learn to appreciate and value individual differences.

4. Attitude is an integral part of tolerance and respect for diversity.

5. Diversity should be an integral part of the college curriculum.

CHAPTER HIGHLIGHTS

CASE STUDY

Pat's New College Friends

Pat spent his entire life in a small, rural community in the northeastern United States. Though his family did not farm, many of his neighbors were dairy farmers who spent every day of the year milking hundreds of dairy cows. As a young child, Pat loved to help the farmers. When he grew older, he was paid to do farm work after school and on weekends. Pat's father owned the local feed store, and his mother was a homemaker. His two younger sisters enjoyed household responsibilities. It was a great place to live and grow up.

Not long after arriving at a large university, Pat wrote a letter to his family describing his college professors. He had a Chinese math professor, a British history professor, a gay economics professor, a female biology professor, and a "seventy-ish" professor for art history. His new roommate, Juan, came from a major city in Puerto Rico. Juan spoke English articulately, but with a slight accent, and liked very different music. Pat and Juan got along fine, but in his letter to his family Pat wrote that he wanted to find a new roommate by next semester or at least by next year.

When Pat entered the university, he wanted to major in accounting. But halfway through his first semester, he started rethinking his choice of a major. To help him determine the right major, he befriended several students with backgrounds similar to his own. He decided that he wanted to be an engineer, since the people in his dorm whom he liked the most were engineering majors. Eventually he would look for a job close to his hometown. Perhaps next semester he would find an engineering major to room with—someone who was more like himself.

If Pat asked you about finding a new roommate who was more like himself, what would you tell him? What do you think about Pat's general approach to life?

Personal Journal

DIVERSITY

Personal Journal 13.1 How do you try to understand others who are different from you? How might John Dewey's attitudes about critical thinking—open-mindedness, wholeheartedness, and responsibility—fit into your understanding of diversity? Explain how you might incorporate these qualities into your daily interactions with others.

_____

_____

_____

_____

_____

_____

_____

_____

DIVERSITY

Personal Journal 13.2 Think of three situations where you encountered an opinion or an activity that exposed you to a totally new concept or behavior. Did you remain open-minded, wholehearted, and responsible in these situations? What impact did your culture, politics, or moral beliefs have on your response? How do you feel about your response? If you had acted with complete open-mindedness, wholeheartedness, and responsibility, how would your response have differed? How would this attitude affect your family? Your friends? Your school? Your community? Your country?

_____

_____

_____

_____

_____

_____

_____

_____

_____

_____

CHAPTER QUIZ

1. What are the major benefits of a diverse society?

_____

_____

_____

_____

_____

2. Describe the major differences between tolerance and respect.

_____

_____

_____

_____

_____

3. Why is Title IX important to higher education?

_____

_____

_____

_____

_____

4. Define the words *open-minded* and *wholehearted* as they apply to attitudes toward diversity.

_____

_____

_____

_____

_____

5. Describe the federal law that equalizes gender participation in college sports.

_____

_____

_____

_____

_____

ADDITIONAL RESOURCES

Dewey, J. *How We Think.* Lexington, MA: D.C. Heath, 1933.

Friedman, Thomas L. *The Lexus and the Olive Tree.* New York: Random House, 1999.

Gelb, M. J. *How to Think Like Leonardo da Vinci.* New York: Delacorte Press, 1998.

Lawrence-Lightfoot, S. *Respect: An Exploration.* Lexington, MA: Perseus Books, 1999.

CHAPTER 14

Building Life Foundations

CHAPTER OBJECTIVES

After reading this chapter, you will understand why:

- This course is important to your success.
- A difference exists between being interested in and being committed to success.
- It is important to be open to change.
- A college education is a critical part of your long-run success.
- It is important to continue your personal growth.

After reading this chapter, you will know how to:

- Use your personal journal to enhance your growth.
- Use your college education to prepare you for a lifetime of learning.
- Keep your dreams alive.
- Continue your personal growth.

This course has taken you on a wonderful adventure of self-discovery on the world's most exciting subject: you. If you applied to your life everything you learned in this course, you are on your way to understanding who you are and what you want to be. This is important to building the foundation for a happy and rewarding life. Remember that what you are building is your life plan. Every day, as you learn more and rethink what you know about yourself and your life, you may change your plan again and again. Your plan will undergo many versions and endless revisions. Your life plan is final only when it is printed in the newspaper as your obituary.

Successful lives result from much reflection and introspective thought. That is why the early part of this course is devoted to developing your sense of self-awareness. The more you understand yourself—your strengths, your weaknesses, your priorities, and what makes you happy—the more likely you will be to achieve your life goals. Life goals are like magnets: They attract your attention and your energies and help you realize your dreams. The secret is to start out with a life plan.

A life plan is a necessary part of achieving a rewarding life. However, the plan itself is not enough. Many people plan on having happy, successful lives, but few are willing to make the personal commitment that will make it happen. Remember, your success is up to you; after all, no one else cares as much about your success as you do. It is your decision to make that commitment to succeed.

▲ Keeping Your Dream Alive

As you move through school and on in life, it is important that you keep the right attitude toward life. As you learned earlier, the right attitude includes being *open-minded* to new ideas and experiences, being *wholehearted* in your commitment to your life goals, and being *responsible* for your actions and their consequences. The right attitude means you are not afraid of new challenges and new situations. It means you are willing to make changes as well as accept changes that come your way. Many people tend to play it safe and not tackle new things. People who are unwilling to tackle the Internet, for example, are missing out on one of the most important changes in world history. With a very small investment of time and sometimes money, they could have access to information that could transform their lives. When you play it safe, you almost always miss out on life's benefits. Life is usually in the process of getting better or getting worse; it seldom stays neutral. It's up to you to make it get better.

Successful people make a commitment to consider all changes. Unsuccessful people are often the ones whose lives are full of "should haves" and "could haves." As William Shakespeare said, "It is better to have loved and lost than never to have loved at all."

▲ Continuing Your Personal Growth

Your life plan and your personal growth do not end when you finish this course. The rest of your life is the next chapter. Hopefully, this course has instilled in you some new habits and some novel ways to look at yourself and the world around you. Much of what you have learned in this course may not be completely new to you, but it should serve as a good reminder and as a new challenge for what you need to do to succeed. If you do something three or four times, it may become a new habit. Success can become that new habit that transforms your life.

ACTIVE LEARNING

Exercise 14.1 *Identify three new study habits that this course has inspired you to adopt.*

_____

_____

_____

_____

_____

CRITICAL THINKING

Exercise 14.2 *What are your goals for next semester? Next year? Five years from now?*

_____

_____

_____

_____

_____

Your personal journal is also a vital ingredient in your personal growth. Continue to write your thoughts and feelings down every day, reflecting on the

things that happen in your life and how you view them. A journal will help you understand your feelings and know what you are thinking. As you look back someday at what you have written, you will be amazed at how you have grown and changed. You will see the big improvements in your life, and you will see how your thoughts have matured. A journal will also help you to keep your mental health on an even keel.

Exercise 14.3 *On a separate sheet of paper, list at least ten questions that you would like to ask an older person whom you consider to be successful. For example, what choices did this person make that influenced his or her life, career, hobbies, family, and so on? Then write three paragraphs describing what you believe were the most important attitudes that influenced this person's life and contributed to his or her success.*

Exercise 14.4 *In a group of three to five, discuss what made each student choose this college. On a separate sheet of paper, create a group list of ten major things that influenced their choices. Rank these influences according to their importance. What is your group's consensus on the top three influences in selecting a college? Then compare your group's rankings with those of the other groups.*

CRITICAL THINKING

Exercise 14.5 *Suppose it is ten years from now. On a separate sheet of paper, write a paragraph that you could use to introduce yourself to a group of your peers. Be sure to include personal and professional information about yourself.*

DIVERSITY

Exercise 14.6 *On a separate sheet of paper, describe in a short essay what you have learned about diversity as a first-year college student. Explain how you have changed (or not changed) your views on diversity.*

CRITICAL THINKING

Exercise 14.7 *Some of your high school friends elected not to go to college. One is working as a server in a fancy restaurant, one is a carpenter for a construction company, one is an auto mechanic, and your best friend is a successful florist. When you return home for a holiday break, your friends want to go out. Describe three things you want to talk about, and explain why you want to talk about these things. On a separate sheet of paper, describe three things you do not want to talk about, and explain why you do not want to talk about them.*

CRITICAL THINKING

Exercise 14.8 *Describe your academic goals for the next semester.*

_____

_____

_____

_____

_____

CRITICAL THINKING

Exercise 14.9 *Before entering college, you planned for a specific major. During your first semester, you learned about a new major that you would like to pursue. Why do you think you are making a good choice? Be specific. How committed are you to your new major?*

_____

_____

_____

_____

CRITICAL THINKING

Exercise 14.10 *List at least three of your major academic interests. Next to each one, write a sentence explaining whether it has a short-term or a long-term value to you and why.*

_____

_____

_____

_____

_____

COLLABORATIVE LEARNING

Exercise 14.11 *Suppose you have chosen a major that is mostly composed of students of the opposite sex. Break up into small groups and make a list of what the most frequently asked questions (FAQs) might be about your choice. Then have group members write down which FAQs personally concern them the most.*

_____

_____

_____

_____

_____

ACTIVE LEARNING

Exercise 14.12 *Identify and describe three people you have met since you started college and how they have helped you in your college experience.*

_____

_____

_____

_____

_____

Exercise 14.13 *On the following chart, describe how each individual listed has changed you or had a positive effect on your college experience.*

How this person	...has changed me	...has strengthened my college experience
Faculty member 1		
Faculty member 2		
Faculty member 3		
Academic adviser		
Roommate		
Friend		
Father		
Mother		
Other		

▲ Learning to Think

Most people look back on their college days as one of the best times in their lives. Many aspects of their college experience contribute to this feeling, but they feel this way largely because college-level learning developed their ability to think for themselves. Here are just some of the positive outcomes of college:

- You develop the ability to analyze.
- You learn to speak and write clearly.
- You discover how to understand what has come before and relate it to what is happening today.
- You learn how to get along with others.
- You see how others live.
- You create a set of personal values.
- You learn about things you never knew existed.
- You become a responsible, thinking adult and citizen.

All of these skills and more form the foundation for a successful and rewarding life. College can positively transform your life and help you reach your life goals. As you get older, you will continue to realize the profound effect college has had on you and how grateful you are for the experience. Many call it the greatest gift they ever received.

▲ Commencement of Lifelong Learning

One of the more enduring benefits of college-level learning is that it prepares you for a pattern of lifelong learning. In college, you not only absorb a body of facts and knowledge but also acquire the ability to learn independently. College prepares you to tackle just about any subject on your own. Graduation day is often called *commencement* because it is the beginning of a lifetime: the start of lifelong learning. Whether you are in a formal classroom setting with a professor or sitting alone at your computer, thinking on your own and making informed decisions are important to you, to your success, and to the future of our democracy.

Leo C. Rosten, noted author, said, "I cannot believe that the purpose of life is to be 'happy.' I think the purpose of life is to be useful, to be responsible, to be honorable, to be compassionate. It is, above all, to matter; to count, to stand for something, to have made a difference that you lived at all."[1]

Your purpose in life is important, and it is attainable. It is up to you to choose to achieve your purpose and your goals.

CHAPTER HIGHLIGHTS

1. The material in this book is the next step on your journey of personal discovery.
2. Successful lives result from reflection, introspective thought, and a strong sense of self-awareness.
3. Having goals makes you more likely to accomplish things.
4. A life plan and a personal commitment to that plan are essential to success.
5. Recognize that change is inevitable.
6. Always be open to new ideas.
7. Continue your personal growth after this course by keeping a personal journal.
8. The greatest gift from a college education is the ability to think.
9. College prepares you to commence lifelong learning.
10. Your future depends on your ability to think and your commitment to success.

CHAPTER HIGHLIGHTS

1. Leo C. Rosten, speech delivered at the National Book Awards, March 1962, New York, NY. Reprinted in *Library Journal*, June 4, 1962, p. 2075.

CASE STUDY
Leah's Little Sister's Questions

The last time Leah was home from college, her little sister asked her two questions:

1. What is college like?
2. What should I do to be successful?

If you were Leah, how would you answer your little sister's questions? What is the best advice you could give her?

Personal Journal

Personal Journal 14.1 Reread your personal journal entries from Chapters 1 and 2. Describe how you have changed since you wrote those journal entries. How have you grown personally? Academically? Socially? Based on what you have learned in this course, how do you think next semester will be different? Be specific in your answer.

_____

_____

_____

_____

_____

_____

_____

_____

CHAPTER QUIZ

1. Why are goals important when you want to accomplish something?

_____

_____

_____

_____

_____

2. Is a plan enough to guarantee success? Explain your answer.

_____

_____

_____

_____

_____

3. Explain the following quotation: "It is better to have loved and lost than never to have loved at all." How does this statement apply to your life goals?

_____

_____

_____

_____

_____

4. Explain why a personal journal helps you continue your personal growth.

_____

_____

_____

_____

5. What is one of the greatest benefits of a college education?

_____

_____

_____

_____

_____

6. Why is graduation often called *commencement*?

_____

_____

_____

_____

_____

Index